In Search of

GOD'S
PERFECTION

In Search of
GOD'S
PERFECTION

ANDREW MURRAY

WHITAKER
HOUSE

Unless otherwise indicated, all Scripture quotations are taken from the King James Version of the Holy Bible. Scripture quotations marked (ASV) are taken from the American Standard Edition of the Revised Version of the Holy Bible.

Publisher's Note: This book has been edited for the modern reader. Words, expressions, and sentence structure have been updated for clarity and readability.

Boldface type in the Scripture quotations indicates the author's emphasis.

IN SEARCH OF GOD'S PERFECTION

(Previously published as *The Secret of God's Presence, How to Be Perfect,* and *God's Gift of Perfection.*)

ISBN: 978-1-60374-974-9
eBook ISBN: 978-1-60374-990-9
Printed in the United States of America
© 1982 by Whitaker House

Whitaker House
1030 Hunt Valley Circle
New Kensington, PA 15068
www.whitakerhouse.com

1 2 3 4 5 6 7 8 9 10 11 ᴜᴜ 21 20 19 18 17 16 15 14

CONTENTS

PREFACE

If anyone picks up this volume with the intention of finding a theory of perfection expounded or vindicated, he will be disappointed. My objective has been a very different one. What I have wished to do is to go with my reader through the Word of God, noting the principal passages in which the word *perfect* occurs, and seeking in each case to find what impression the word was meant to convey from its context. It is only when we have yielded ourselves—simply and prayerfully—to allow the words of Scripture to have their full force that we are on the right track for combining the different aspects of truth into one harmonious whole.

Among the thoughts which have especially been brought home to me in these meditations, and with which I trust my readers will agree, the following are the most important:

1. *There is a perfection which Scripture speaks of as possible and attainable.* There may be, rather, there is, great diversity of opinion as to how the term is to be defined. But there can be only one opinion as to the fact that God asks and expects His children to be perfect with

Him. There is only one opinion in relation to the fact that He promises perfection as His own work and that Scripture speaks of some as having been perfect before Him—having served Him with a perfect heart. Scripture speaks of a perfection that is at once our duty and our hope.

2. *To know what this perfection is, we must begin by accepting the command and obeying it with our whole heart.* Our natural tendency is to do the very opposite. We want to discuss and define what perfection is to understand how the command can be reconciled with our assured conviction that no man is perfect and to provide for all the dangers we are sure to find in the path of perfection.

This is not God's way. Jesus said, *"If any man will **do** his will, he shall **know**"* (John 7:17). The same principle holds true in all human attainment. It is only he who has accepted the command *"Be ye therefore perfect"* (Matthew 5:48) in adoring submission and obedience who can hope to know what that perfection is. Until the church is seen prostrate before God, seeking this blessing as the highest good, it will be no wonder if the very word *perfection*—instead of being an attraction and a joy—is a cause of apprehension and anxiety, of division and offense. May God increase the number of those who, in childlike humility, take the Word from His own lips as a living seed, in the assurance that it will bring forth much fruit.

3. *Perfection is no arbitrary demand; in the very nature of things, God can ask nothing less. And this is true, whether we think of Him or of ourselves.* If we think of God, who has created the universe for Himself and His glory, who

alone is able to fill it with His happiness and love, then we can see how impossible it is for Him to share man's heart with anything other than Himself. God must be all and have all. As Lawgiver and Judge, He dare not be content with anything less than absolute, legal perfection. As Redeemer and Father, it equally becomes Him to claim nothing less than a real, childlike perfection. God must have all.

If we think of ourselves, the call to perfection is no less absolutely necessary. God is an infinite, spiritual good, and the soul is incapable of receiving or knowing or enjoying Him unless it gives itself wholly to Him. For our own sakes, God's love can demand of us nothing less than a perfect heart.

4. *Perfection, as the highest aim of what God in His great power would do for us, is something so divine, spiritual, and heavenly that it is only the soul that yields itself very tenderly to the leading of the Holy Spirit that can know its blessedness.* God has given every human heart a deep desire for perfection. That desire is manifested in the admiration that all men have for excellence in the different objects or pursuits to which they attach value. In the believer who yields himself wholly to God, this desire fastens itself upon God's wonderful promises and inspires a prayer like that of M'Cheyne: "Lord, make me as holy as a pardoned sinner can be made." The more we learn to long for this full conformity to God's will—for the consciousness that we are always pleasing to Him—the more we will see that all this must come as a gift directly from heaven, as the full birth in us of the life of God. This happens we those who are wholly yielded to God

inbreathe the Holy Spirit of Jesus. Trusting ever less to men's thoughts and teachings, we will often retire into the secret of God's presence, with the assurance that the more we see God's face and hear the secret voice that comes directly from Him—*"Be ye therefore perfect"*—the more the Holy Spirit dwelling within us will unfold the heavenly fullness and power of the words. He will make them, as God's Word says, bring and give and work the very thing He speaks.

In the hope that these simple meditations may help some of God's children to go on to perfection, I commit them and myself to the blessed Father's teaching and keeping.

—Andrew Murray

PRAYER

Ever blessed Father! You have sent me a message by your beloved Son that I am to be perfect as You are perfect. Coming from You, incomprehensible and most glorious God, it means more than man can grasp. Coming to You, I ask that You would teach me what it means, work in me what it claims, and give me what it promises.

My Father, I accept the Word in the obedience of faith. I yield my life to its rule. I hide it in my heart as a living seed, in the assurance that there, deeper than thought or feeling, Your Holy Spirit can make it take root and grow up.

And as I go through Your Word, to meditate on what it says about the path of the perfect, teach me, O my Father, to bring every thought of mine captive to the obedience of Christ and to wait for that teaching of Your Holy Spirit which is so sure to the upright in heart. Through Him You have sent me this message, give me the answer to this prayer, too. Amen.

1

A PERFECT HEART

*Noah was a just man and perfect in his generations, and
Noah walked with God.*
—Genesis 6:9

*And the LORD said unto Satan, Hast thou considered my
servant Job, that there is none like him in the earth,
a perfect and an upright man, one that feareth God,
and escheweth evil?*
—Job 1:8

*[Solomon's] heart was not perfect with the LORD his God,
as was the heart of David his father.*
—1 Kings 11:4

Asa's heart was perfect with the LORD all his days.
—1 Kings 15:14

Concerning the above four men, Holy Scripture testifies that
they were perfect, or that their hearts were perfect with God.

Scripture also testifies that each of them were not perfect in the sense of absolute sinlessness. We know how Noah fell. We know how Job had to humble himself before God. We know how sadly David sinned. And of Asa, we read that there came a time when he acted foolishly and relied on the Syrians and not on the Lord his God. In his disease, he did not seek the Lord but the physicians. And yet the hearts of these men were perfect with the Lord their God.

To understand this, there is one thing we must remember. The meaning of the word *perfect* must be decided, in each case, by that particular stage in God's education of His people in which it is used. What a father or a teacher regards as perfection in a child of ten years is very different from what he would call perfection in one of twenty years. As to the attitude or spirit, the perfection would be the same. In its content, however, by which it was to be judged, there would be a great difference.

We will see later on how, in the Old Testament, nothing was really made perfect. We will see how Christ has come to reveal and work out and impart true perfection in His people. We will also see how perfection, as revealed in the New Testament, is something infinitely higher, more spiritual and effective, than that which was under the old system. And yet, at the root, they are one. God looks at the heart. A heart that is perfect with Him is an object of complacency and approval. A wholehearted consecration to His will and fellowship, a life that takes as its motto Wholly for God, has been in all ages—even where the Spirit had not yet been given entrance into the heart—accepted by God as the mark of the perfect man.

The lesson these Scriptures suggest to us is a very simple, yet very searching, one. In God's record of the lives of His servants, there are some of whom it is written: his heart was perfect with the Lord his God. Let each reader ask, is this what God sees and says of me? Does my life, in the sight of God, bear the mark of intense, wholehearted consecration to God's will and service? Does my life burn with the desire to be as perfect as it is possible for grace to make me? Let us yield ourselves to the searching light of this question. Let us believe that with this word *perfect*, God means something very real and true. Let us not evade its force or hide ourselves from its condemning power by the vain excuse that we do not fully know what it means. Before we can understand it, we must first accept it and give up our lives to it. I cannot stress too strongly that, whether in the church at large and its teaching or in the life of the individual believer, there can be no hope of comprehending what perfection is except as we count all things loss to be apprehended by it, to live for it, to accept it, and to possess it.

But there is only so much we can understand. What I do with a perfect heart I do with love and delight, with a willing mind and all my strength. It implies a definite purpose and a concentrated effort, which makes everything subordinate to the one object of my choice. This is what God asks, what His saints have given, and what we must give.

Again I say to everyone who wishes to join me in seeking perfection, through the Word of God, the revelation of His will concerning perfection: Yield yourself to the searching question, "Can God say of me as He did of Noah and Job, of David and Asa—that my heart is perfect with the Lord my God? Have I given myself up to say that there must be nothing, nothing whatever, to share my heart with God and His will? Is a heart perfect with the Lord my God the object of my desire, my prayer, my faith, my hope?"

Whether it has been so or not, let it be so today. Make this promise of God's Word your own: *"The very God of peace sanctify you wholly"* (1 Thessalonians 5:23). God, who has the power to do more than we ask or think, will open up to you the blessed hope of a life, of which He says, "His heart was perfect with the Lord his God."

2

WALK BEFORE ME

*And when Abram was ninety years old and nine, the
LORD appeared to Abram, and said unto him, I am the
Almighty God; walk before me, and be thou perfect.
And I will make my covenant between me and thee, and
will multiply thee exceedingly. And Abram fell on his face:
and God talked with him.*
—Genesis 17:1–3

Thou shalt be perfect with the LORD thy God.
—Deuteronomy 18:13

It had been twenty-four years since God had called Abraham
to go out from his father's home and he obeyed. In those years,
he had been a learner in the school of faith. The time was
approaching for him to inherit the promise, and God came to
establish His covenant with him. In view of this, God met him
with this threefold word: *"I am the Almighty God; walk before
me, and be thou perfect"* (Genesis 17:1).

"Be thou perfect." The context in which we find the word *perfect* will help us to understand its meaning. God reveals Himself

as God Almighty. Abraham's faith had long been tried, and it was about to achieve one of its greatest triumphs—faith was to be changed to vision in the birth of Isaac. God invites Abraham more than ever to remember His promise and to rest upon His omnipotence. He is Almighty God; all things are possible to Him; He holds rule over all. All of His power is working for those who trust Him. And all He asks of Abraham is that he be perfect with Him—give Him his whole heart, his perfect confidence.

Likewise, God Almighty, with all His power, is wholly for you. Be thou wholly for God. The knowledge and faith of what God is lies at the root of what we are to be: "*I am the Almighty God...be thou perfect.*" As I know Him whose power fills heaven and earth, I see that this is the one thing we need—to be perfect with Him, wholly and entirely given up to Him. To be wholly for God is the keynote of perfection.

"*Walk before me, and be thou perfect.*" It is in the life of fellowship with God, in His realized presence and favor, that it becomes possible to be perfect with Him. He said, "*Walk before me.*" Abraham had been doing this. God's Word called him to a clearer and more conscious understanding of this as his life calling.

It is easy for us to study what Scripture says of perfection, to form our ideas of it, and to argue for them. But let us remember that it is only as we are walking closely with God, seeking, and in some measure attaining, uninterrupted communion with Him that the divine command will come to us in its divine power. Only then will it unfold to us its divine meaning. "*Walk before me, and be thou perfect.*" God's realized presence is the school—the secret—of perfection. It is only he who studies what perfection is in the full light of God's presence to whom its hidden glory will be opened up that truly understands what it means.

That realized presence is the great blessing of the redemption in Jesus Christ. The veil has been torn; the way into the true sanctuary, the presence of God, has been opened. We can enter with boldness the Holiest place of all. God, who has proved Himself God Almighty in raising Jesus from the dead and setting Him at His right hand, speaks now to us: *"I am the Almighty God; walk before me, and be thou perfect."*

That command did not come only to Abraham; Moses gave it to the whole people of Israel: *"Thou shalt be perfect with the* Lord *thy God."* This command is for all Abraham's children, for all the people Israel of God, and *for every believer.* Oh! do not think that before you can obey, you must first understand and define what perfection means. No, God's way is the exact opposite of this. Abraham went out, *"not knowing whither he went"* (Hebrews 11:8). You are called to go on to perfection: go out, not knowing where you go. It is a land God will show you. Let your heart be filled with His glory: *"I am the Almighty God."* Let your life be spent in His presence: *"Walk before me."* As His power and His presence rest upon you and fill you, your heart, before you know it, will be drawn up and strengthened to accept and rejoice in and fulfill the command: *"Be thou perfect."* As surely as the opening bud has only to abide in the light of the sun to attain perfection, so the soul that walks in the light of God will attain perfection, too. As the God who is all shines upon it, it cannot but rejoice to give Him all.

3

PERFECT WITH THE LORD

Thou shalt be perfect with the LORD thy God.
—Deuteronomy 18:13

To be perfect before God is not only the call and the privilege of men like Abraham, it is equally the duty of all His children. The command is given to all of Israel, for each man of God's people to receive and obey: *"Thou shalt be perfect with the LORD thy God"* (Deuteronomy 18:13). It comes to each child of God. No one professing to be a Christian may turn away from it or refuse to obey it without endangering his salvation. It is not a command like, *"Thou shalt not kill"* (Exodus 20:13) or, *"Thou shalt not steal"* (verse 15), referencing a limited part of our life; instead, it is a principle that lies at the very root of all true Christianity. If our service to God is to be acceptable, it must not be with a divided heart but with a whole, perfect heart.

The chief hindrance to obedience of this command lies in our misunderstanding of what Christianity really is. Man was created to simply live for God and to show forth His glory by allowing God to show how completely He could reveal His likeness and blessedness in man. God lives for man, longing in the greatness of His love to communicate His goodness and His love to him. It was for this life, lost by sin, that Christ came to

21

redeem us back. The selfishness of the human heart makes it look at salvation as simply an escape from hell, with as much holiness as needed to make its happiness secure. Christ meant for us to be restored to the state from which we had fallen—the whole heart, the whole will, the whole life given up to the glory and service of God. To be wholly given up to God, to be perfect with the Lord our God, lies at the very root of Christianity; it is the very essence of true faith. The enthusiastic devotion of the whole heart to God is what is asked of us.

When the misconception of salvation has been removed and the truth begins to dawn on the soul, a second hindrance is generally met in relation to unbelief: How can these things be? Instead of first accepting God's command and then waiting in the path of obedience for the teaching of the Spirit, men are at once ready with their own interpretation of the Word and confidently affirm that it cannot be. They forget what the whole object of the gospel and the glory of Christ's redemption is— that it makes possible what is beyond man's thoughts or powers. It reveals God not as a Lawgiver and Judge, exacting the uttermost penny, but as a Father, who graciously deals with each one according to his or her capacity, accepting the devotion and the intention of the heart.

We understand this of an earthly father. A child of ten is doing some little service for the father, helping him in his work. The work of the child is very defective, and yet it is a cause of joy and hope to the father. The father sees in it the proof of the child's attachment and obedience and understands what the child's devotion will do for him, the father, when his intelligence and his strength have been increased. The child has served the father with a perfect heart, though the perfect heart does not at once imply perfect work. Even so, our Father in heaven accepts as a perfect heart the simple, childlike one who makes His reverence and service its one object. The Christian may be deeply humbled at the involuntary uprisings of the evil nature. But God's Spirit teaches him to say, *"It is no more I that do it, but sin that dwelleth in me"* (Romans 7:17). He may be sorely grieved by the consciousness of shortcoming and failure, but he hears the voice of Jesus, *"The spirit indeed is willing, but the flesh is weak"* (Matthew 26:41). Even as Christ counted the love and obedience of His faithless disciples as such and accepted their effort as the condition on which He had promised them His Spirit, so the Christian can receive the witness of the Spirit, knowing that the Father sees and accepts in him the perfect heart. It can be so even where there is not yet perfect performance.

"Thou shalt be perfect with the LORD *thy God."* O let us beware of making the Word of God too little effect by our traditions! Let us believe the message, *"Ye are not under the law, but under grace"* (Romans 6:14). Let us realize what grace is in its pitying tenderness: *"As a father pitieth his children, so the* LORD *pitieth them that fear him"* (Psalm 103:13) and what it is in its mighty power working in us both to will and to do: *"The God of all grace…*[shall] *make you perfect"* (1 Peter 5:10). If we hold fast our integrity, our confidence, and our hope, steadfast unto the end, being perfect in heart will lead us on to be perfect in the way. And we will realize that Christ also fulfills His perfection in us, for *"*[we] *shalt be perfect with the* LORD [our] *God."*

4

WALK WITH A PERFECT HEART

*Then he turned his face to the wall, and prayed
unto the L*ORD*, saying, I beseech thee, O L*ORD*,
remember now how I have walked before thee in truth and
with a perfect heart, and have done that which is good in
thy sight. And Hezekiah wept sore. And it came to pass,
afore Isaiah was gone out into the middle court,
that the word of the L*ORD *came to him, saying,
Turn again, and tell Hezekiah the captain of my people,
Thus saith the L*ORD*, the God of David thy father,
I have heard thy prayer, I have seen thy tears.*
—2 Kings 20:2–5

What a childlike simplicity of communication with God. When the Son was about to die, He said, *"I have glorified thee on the earth: I have finished the work which thou gavest me to do. And now, O Father, glorify thou me"* (John 17:4–5). He pleaded His life and work as the grounds for expecting an answer to His prayer. And so Hezekiah, the servant of God, also pleaded, not as a matter of merit, but in the confidence that *"God is not unrighteous to forget your work* [of faith] *and labour of*

25

love" (Hebrews 6:10). He knew that God would remember how he had walked before Him with a perfect heart.

The words first of all suggest to us that the man who walks before God with a perfect heart can know it—it may be a matter of consciousness. Let us look at the testimony Scripture gives of Hezekiah: *"He did that which was right in the sight of the* Lord, *according to all that David his father did"* (2 Kings 18:3). Then follow the different elements of this his that was right in God's sight: *"He trusted in the* Lord *God of Israel....For he clave to the* Lord, *and departed not from following him, but kept his command-ments, which the* Lord *commanded Moses"* (2 Kings 18:5–6). His life was one of trust and love, of steadfastness and obedi-ence. And the Lord was with him. He was one of the saints who *"obtained a good report through faith"* (Hebrews 11:39). He had the witness that he was righteous, that he was pleasing to God.

Let us seek to have this blessed consciousness. Paul had it when he wrote,

> *For our rejoicing is this, the testimony of our conscience, that in simplicity and godly sincerity, not with fleshly wisdom, but by the grace of God, we have had our conversation in the world, and more abundantly to you-ward.*
> (2 Corinthians 1:12)

John had this consciousness when he said,

> *Beloved, if our heart condemn us not, then have we con-fidence toward God. And whatsoever we ask, we receive of him, because we keep his commandments, and do those things that are pleasing in his sight.* (1 John 3:21–22)

If we are to have perfect peace and confidence, if we are to walk in the holy boldness and the blessed glory of which

Scripture speaks, we must know that our heart is perfect with God.

Hezekiah's prayer suggests a second lesson—that the consciousness of a perfect heart gives wonderful power to prayer. Read again the words of his prayer and notice how his plea is to walk with a perfect. Read again the words just quoted from John and see how clearly he says that those who obey God will receive of Him whatever they ask. It is a heart that does not condemn us, which knows that it is perfect toward God, that gives us boldness.

Probably every reader of these lines can painfully testify how, at some time or other, his or her knowledge of his or her imperfection has hindered confidence and prayer. And, mistaken views as to what the perfect heart means, as well as the danger of becoming self-righteous when praying Hezekiah's prayer, have in very many cases banished all possibility of attaining that boldness and confident assurance of receiving an answer to prayer, which John connects with a heart that does not condemn us.

Oh! that we would give up all our prejudices and learn to take God's Word as it stands—the only rule of our faith; the only measure of our expectations. Our daily prayers would be reminders that God asks for a perfect heart. They would be a new occasion of childlike confession as to our walking or not walking with a perfect heart before God, and a new motive to make nothing less than fellowship with our Father in heaven our standard. How our boldness in God's presence would be ever clearer. How our consciousness of His acceptance would be brighter. How the humbling thought of our nothingness be quickened and our assurance of His strength in our weakness and His answer to prayers become the joy of life.

Oh! the comfort we receive amid all consciousness of imperfection! We are able to say, in childlike simplicity, "Remember, O Lord, how I have walked before Thee with a perfect heart."

5

GOD GIVES A
PERFECT HEART

*Give unto Solomon my son a perfect heart, to keep thy
commandments, thy testimonies, and thy statutes.*
—1 Chronicles 29:19

*Let my heart be sound in thy statutes;
that I be not ashamed.*
—Psalm 119:80

David, in his parting commission, laid it upon Solomon to serve God with a perfect heart, because God searches the heart. It is nothing less than the whole heart, a perfect heart, that God wants. Very shortly after David's dedication prayer, after the giving of all the material for the temple, He returns again to the subject of a pure heart as the one thing that is needed and asks it for his son as a gift from God. *"Give unto Solomon my son a perfect heart"* (1 Chronicles 29:19). The perfect heart is a gift from God, given and received under the laws which rule all His giving. It is given as a hidden seed to be accepted and acted on in faith.

The command *"Be ye therefore perfect"* (Matthew 5:48) comes and claims immediate and full submission. Where this submission is yielded, the need for divine power to work it into our hearts becomes our motivation for urgent and earnest prayer. The word of command, received and hid in a good and honest heart, becomes the seed of this divine power. God works His grace in us by stirring us to work. So the desire to listen to God's command and to serve Him with a perfect heart is a desire that God instills, and that which He will strengthen and perfect. The gift of a perfect heart is thus obtained in the way of obedience of faith. Begin at once to serve God with a perfect heart, and the perfect heart will be given to you.

The perfect heart is a gift from God; it is to be asked for and obtained by prayer. No one will pray for it earnestly, persever-ingly, or believingly until he accepts God's Word fully that to be perfect is a positive command and an immediate duty. Where this has been done, the consciousness of the utter impossibil-ity of attempting obedience in human strength will soon grow strong. And faith that the word of command was simply meant to draw the soul to Him who gives to us what He asks from us will grow.

Once this faith is secured, the perfect heart must be obtained in prayer. David asked the Lord to give it to his son, Solomon, even as he had prayed for himself long before, *"Let my heart be perfect in thy statutes"* (Psalm 119:80 ASV). Let all of us who long for this blessing follow David's example. Let us make it a matter of definite, earnest prayer. Let each son and daughter of God ask of the Father, "Give Your child a perfect heart."

Let us, in the course of our meditations in this book, turn each word of command or teaching or promise into prayer— pointed, personal prayer that asks and claims, accepts and proves the gift of a perfect heart. When the seed begins to root and the Spirit gives the consciousness that the beginning of the perfect heart has been bestowed with the wholehearted purpose to live for God alone, then let us hold on in prayer for the perfect heart in all its completeness.

A heart perfect in its purpose toward God—this is only the initial stage. Then there comes the putting on of one grace after another—the going on from strength to strength to perfection—the putting on, in ever-growing distinctness of likeness, the Lord Jesus, with every trait of His holy image. All this is to be sought and found in prayer, too. He who understands what is perfect in purpose will pray to be perfect in practice, as well.

From the words of Hezekiah, we see that there are two elements to a perfect heart: a relationship to God and an obedience to His commandments. Hezekiah said to the Lord, *"I have walked before thee in truth and with a perfect heart, and have done that which is good in thy sight"* (2 Kings 20:3). David speaks of the latter in his prayer, *"Give unto Solomon my son **a perfect heart**, to keep thy commandments."* The two always go together—walking with God will ensure us walking in His commandments.

"Every good gift and every perfect gift is from above, and cometh down from the Father of lights" (James 1:17)—this includes the gift of a perfect heart, too. James instructed us to *"ask [of Christ] in faith, nothing wavering"* (James 1:6). Let us be sure that in the believing, adoring worship of God, there will be given to the soul that is set upon having it nothing less than what God Himself meant by a perfect heart. Let us pray the prayer boldly: "Lord, give Your child a perfect heart. Let my heart be perfect in Your statutes."

6

STRENGTHEN THE PERFECT HEART

Were not the Ethiopians and the Lubims a huge host,
with very many chariots and horsemen? yet, because thou
didst rely on the LORD, he delivered them into thine hand.
For the eyes of the LORD run to and fro throughout the
whole earth, to show himself strong in the behalf of them
whose heart is perfect toward him.
—2 Chronicles 16:8–9

We have here the same three thoughts we had in God's words to Abraham. There, it was the *command* to be perfect in connection with *faith* in God's power and a *walk* in His presence. Here, the perfect heart is spoken of as the condition of the experience of God's power and as that which His eyes seek and approve of. The words teach us the great lesson of the value of the perfect heart in His sight. It is the one thing He longs for. To find such, *"The eyes of the LORD run to and fro throughout the whole earth"* (1 Chronicles 16:9). The Father seeks such to worship Him. And when He finds them, He shows Himself strong in their behalf. It is the one thing that shows that the soul has the capacity of receiving and showing forth God's glory and strength.

The context proves that the chief mark of the perfect heart is trust in God. *"Because thou didst rely on the* LORD, *he delivered them into thine hand. For the eyes of the* LORD *run to and fro throughout the whole earth, to show himself strong in the behalf of them whose heart is perfect toward him"* (2 Chronicles 16:8–9). The essence of faith is this: it gives God His place and glory as God. Relying on Him alone allows Him free room to work. It lets God be God. In such faith or reliance, the heart proves itself perfect toward God. With no other object of confidence or desire, the heart and soul depend on none but Him. As the eyes of God go to and fro throughout the world, wherever He discovers such a man, He delights to prove Himself strong for him. He desires to work for him or in him, as the case may be, according to the riches of the glory of His power.

What precious lessons these words teach us for the Christian's life. To have God reveal His strength in us, to have Him make us strong for life or work, for doing or for suffering, *our heart must be perfect with Him.* Let us not shrink from accepting this truth. Let no preconceived notion of the impossibility of perfection keep us from allowing the Word of God to have its full effect upon us. He shows Himself strong to those whose heart is perfect toward Him. Before we attempt to define a perfect heart, let us first receive the truth that there *is* such a thing as what God calls a perfect heart. Let us say it will be ours. Let us rest contented with nothing short of knowing that the eyes of the Lord have seen that we are wholeheartedly with Him. Let us not be afraid to say, *"With my whole heart have I sought thee"* (Psalm 119:10).

We saw how the chief mark of this perfect heart is reliance on God. God looks for men who trust Him fully—in them, He will show His power. God is a being of infinite and incomprehensible glory and power. Our mind cannot form a proper conception of what He can do for us. Even when we have His Word and promises, our human thoughts of what He means are always defective. By nothing do we dishonor God more than by limiting Him. By nothing do we limit Him more than by allowing our human ideas of what He proposes to be the measure of our expectations. The reliance of a heart perfect toward Him is simply this: it yields to Him as God; it rests upon Him; it allows Him, as God, to do in His own way what He has promised. The heart is perfect toward Him in meeting Him with a perfect faith for all that He is and does as God. Faith expects from God what is beyond all expectation.

The Father seeks such people. Oh! with what joy He finds them. How He delights in them as His eyes, running to and fro throughout the world, rest upon them to show Himself as their strong and mighty Helper! Let us walk before God with a perfect heart, relying on Him to work in us above all that we can ask or think. The one great need of the spiritual life is to know that it is entirely dependent upon God to work in it. The follower of Christ must know the exceeding greatness of God's power that is in him. As the soul knows this, and with a perfect heart yields to Almighty God to let Him do His work within, oh! how strong He will show Himself in its behalf.

7

GOD HIMSELF PERFECT

I was also perfect with him, and I kept myself from mine iniquity.
—Psalm 18:23 (ASV)

With the perfect man thou wilt show thyself perfect.
—Psalm 18:25 (ASV)

As for God, his way is perfect: the word of the LORD is tried: he is a buckler to all those that trust in him.
—Psalm 18:30

It is God that girdeth me with strength, and maketh my way perfect.
—Psalm 18:32

As for God, his way is perfect" (Psalm 18:30). In all He does and in all He is, He is perfect. God is the perfection of goodness and beauty. In nature and grace, in heaven and on earth, in the greatest and in the least, everything that is in God and of God—down to the very hem of His garment—is infinite perfection. Men who study and admire the perfection of His works, saints who love and seek the perfection of His service and fellowship, see that perfection can only be found in God Himself! As for God, His way is perfect—this is the highest we can say of Him, though we can comprehend but little of it.

"He maketh my way perfect" (Psalm 18:32). Of God's perfection, this is the chief excellence—that He does not keep it for Himself; heaven and earth are full of His glory. God is love, who lives not for Himself but in the energy of an infinite life. He makes His creatures, as far as they can possibly receive it, partakers of His perfection. It is His delight to perfect all around Him. It is especially His delight to perfect the soul of the man who rises up to Him. God would have perfect harmony between His servant and Himself. The Father wants the child to be as Himself. The more I learn in adoring worship to say, *"As for God, his way is perfect"* (verse 30) the sooner I will have the faith and grace of the psalmist to say, *"[He] maketh my way perfect"* (verse 32).

As we believe this—that is, receive the heavenly truth of these words into our inmost being and absorb them—we will not wonder that the same man also said, *"I was also perfect with him, and I kept myself from mine iniquity"* (Psalm 18:23 ASV); *"It is God that girdeth me with strength…maketh my way perfect"* (Psalm 18:32). He alone has the power and the honor and the glory of what He has worked. This makes the confession *"I was also perfect with him"* (verse 23 ASV) so far from being presumption or self-righteousness. It is nothing but an act of praise to Him to whom it is due.

And then follow the words in which the perfection of God and that of man are seen in their wonderful relationship and harmony: *"With the perfect man thou wilt show thyself perfect"* (Psalm 18:26 ASV). Just as there can be no light of day except that which comes from the sun, so there can be no perfection except that which comes from God. God's perfection wrestles with man in its feeblest beginnings in the soul, so as to break through and get possession. As long as man refuses to consent, God cannot make His perfection known, for God must be to us what we are to Him: *"With the perverse thou wilt show thyself froward"* (verse 26 ASV). But where man's will consents, and his heart chooses this perfection and this perfect God as its portion, God meets the soul with even larger manifestations of how perfect He is toward His own. *"With the perfect man thou wilt show thyself perfect"* (verse 26 ASV).

Christian, walk before God with a perfect heart, and you will experience how perfect the heart and the love and the will of God is toward you. God will take perfect possession of a heart perfectly yielded to Him. Walk before God in a perfect way, and your eyes and heart will be opened to see, in adoring wonder, how perfect God's way is. Mightily take hold of this word as the law of God's revelation of Himself: *"With the perfect man thou wilt show thyself perfect"* (Psalm 18:26 ASV). To a soul perfectly devoted to Him, God will wonderfully reveal Himself.

Turn with your whole heart and life, your whole trust and obedience, toward God. Walk before Him with a perfect heart, and He will show Himself perfect to you. God, whose way is perfect, makes your way perfect, and He perfects you in every good thing. When you say, *"With my whole heart have I sought thee"* (Psalm 119:10), He will answer you with, *"Yea, I will rejoice over* [you] *to do* [you] *good...with my whole heart and with my whole soul"* (Jeremiah 32:41). Oh! say it in faith and hope and joy, *"With the perfect man thou wilt show thyself perfect"* (Psalm 18:25 asv).

8

PERFECT IN HEART

Blessed are they that are perfect in the way,
who walk in the law of Jehovah. Blessed are they that keep
his testimonies, that seek him with the whole heart.
—Psalm 119:1–2 (ASV)

Let my heart be perfect in thy statutes,
that I be not put to shame.
—Psalm 119:80 (ASV)

I will behave myself wisely in a perfect way.
O when wilt thou come unto me? I will walk within my
house with a perfect heart.
—Psalm 101:2

We have seen what Scripture says of the perfect heart. Here it speaks of the perfect walk. *"Blessed are they that are perfect in the way, who walk in the law of Jehovah"* (Psalm 119:1 ASV). These are the opening words of the beautiful psalm which I can say, from personal experience, depicts the wonderful blessedness of a life in the law and the will of God. As he looks back upon the past, the psalmist does not hesitate to claim that he has kept that law. *"I have kept thy testimonies"* (Psalm 119:22); *"I have... kept thy law"* (verse 55); *"I forsook not thy precepts"* (verse 87); *"I have not departed from thy judgments"* (verse 102); *"I have done judgment and justice"* (verse 121); *"I have not swerved from thy testimonies"* (verse 157 asv); *"I have...done thy commandments"* (verse 166); *"My soul hath kept thy testimonies"* (verse 167). May the man who can look up to God and, in simplicity of soul, speak thus, say, "[How] *blessed are they that are perfect in the way"* (Psalm 119:1 asv)!

What is meant by being *"perfect in the way"* (Psalm 119:1 asv) becomes plain as we study the psalm. Perfection includes two elements. First, the perfection of heart—the earnestness of purpose with which a man gives himself up to seek God and His will. Second, the perfection of obedience, in which a man seeks not only to do some, but all, of the commandments of his God, and he rests content with nothing less than the New Testament privilege of *"stand[ing] perfect and complete in all the will of God"* (Colossians 4:12).

The psalmist speaks of both with great confidence. Hear how he testifies of the former in words such as these: *"Blessed are they...that seek him with the whole heart"* (Psalm 119:2); *"With my whole heart have I sought thee"* (verse 10); *"I shall observe* [the law] *with my whole heart"* (verse 34); *"I will keep thy precepts with my whole heart"* (verse 69); *"Thy law had been my delights"* (verse 92); *"O how love I thy law!"* (verse 97); *"Consider how I love thy precepts"* (verse 159); *"I love them exceedingly"* (verse 167). This is indeed the perfect heart of which we have already heard. The whole psalm is a prayer, an appeal to God Himself to consider and see how His servant, in wholehearted simplicity, has chosen God and His law as his only portion.

More than once we have said that the root of all perfection lies in the wholeheartedness of the perfect heart. But it is only the root and beginning. There is another element that must not be neglected. God is to be found in His will. He who would truly find and fully enjoy God must meet Him in all His will. This is not always understood. A man may have his heart intent on serving God perfectly and yet unconscious of how very imperfect his knowledge is of God's will. The very earnestness of his purpose and his consciousness of integrity toward God may deceive him. As far as he knows, he does God's will. But he forgets how much of that blessed will he does not yet know. He can learn a very blessed lesson from the writer of our psalm.

Hear how he speaks: *"I have refrained my feet from every evil way"* (Psalm 119:101); *"I hate every false way"* (verse 104, 128); *"I esteem all thy precepts concerning all things to be right"* (verse 128). It is this surrender to a life of entire and perfect obedience that explains the need he felt of divine teaching and the confidence with which he pleaded for it and expected it. *"Let my heart be perfect in thy statutes"* (Psalm 119:80 asv). The soul that longs for nothing less than to be perfect, and in deep consciousness of its need of a divine teaching, pleads for it, will not be disappointed.

In our next meditation we pass on to the New Testament. In the Old Testament, we have the time of preparation—the awakening of the spirit of holy expectancy—awaiting God's fulfillment of His promises. In the Old Testament, the perfect heart was the vessel, emptied and cleansed for God's filling. In the New Testament, we will find Christ perfected forevermore, who perfects us and fits us to walk perfect in Him. In the New

Testament, the word that looks at the human side, perfect in heart, disappears to give place to that which reveals the divine filling that awaits the prepared vessel: perfect Love; *"[God's] love...perfected in us"* (1 John 4:12).

"Blessed are they that are perfect in the way" (Psalm 119:1 ASV)! We have heard the testimony of an Old Testament saint; and is it not written of New Testament times, *"He that is feeble among them at that day shall be as David"* (Zechariah 12:8)? Surely now, in the fullness of time, when Jesus our High Priest saves completely in the power of an endless life, and the Holy Spirit has come out of God's heaven to dwell within us and be our life, there need not be one word of the psalm that is not meant to be literal truth in the mouth of every believer. Let us read it once more. Speaking it word for word before God as its writer did, we too will begin to sing, *"Blessed are they that are perfect in the way, who...seek him with the whole heart"* (Psalm 119:1 ASV).

9

PERFECT AS THE FATHER

Be ye therefore perfect,
even as your Father which is in heaven is perfect.
—Matthew 5:48

Perfect before God, perfect with God, perfect toward God—these are the expressions we find in the Old Testament. They all indicate a relationship—the choice or purpose of the heart set upon God, the wholehearted desire to trust and obey Him.

The first word of the New Testament at once lifts us to a very different level and opens to us what Christ has brought for us. We are not only to be perfect *toward* God, but perfect *as* God. This is the wonderful prospect it holds out to us. It reveals the infinite fullness of meaning the word *perfect* has in God's mind. At once, it gives us the only standard we are to aim at and to judge by. It casts down all hopes of perfection as a human attainment. Instead, it awakens hope in him who trusts that God has the power, and, as our Father, He has the will to make us like Himself.

A young child may be the perfect image of his father. There may be a great difference in age, in stature, in power; and yet the resemblance may be so striking that everyone notices it. And so a child of God (though infinitely less) may yet bear the image of the Father so markedly, may have such a striking likeness to the Father, that, in his human life, he will be as perfect as the Father is in His divine life. This is possible. It is why Jesus here commands. It is what each one should aim for. *"Perfect, even as your Father which is in heaven is perfect"* (Matthew 5:48) must become one of the first articles of our creed, one of the guiding lights in our Christian life.

What this perfection of the Father consists of is evident from this context:

> But I say unto you, Love your enemies…that ye may be the children of your Father which is in heaven: for he maketh his sun to rise on the evil and on the good, and sendeth rain on the just and on the unjust.…Be ye therefore perfect, even as your Father which is in heaven is perfect.
>
> (Matthew 5:44–45, 48)

Or, as it is says in Luke 6:36, *"Be ye therefore merciful, as your Father also is merciful."* The perfection of God is His love—His will to communicate His own blessedness to all those around Him. His compassion and mercy are the glory of His being. He created us in His image to find our glory in a life of love and mercy and benevolence. It is in love that we are to be perfect, even as our Father is perfect.

The thought that comes up at once, and that always returns again, is this: Is it possible? And if so, how? It certainly does not happen as a fruit of man's efforts. But the words themselves contain the answer: *"perfect, **even as your Father**…is perfect"* (Matthew 5:48). It is because the little child has received his life from his father, and because the father watches over his training and development, that there can be such a striking and ever-increasing resemblance between the child in his feebleness and the father in his strength. It is because the sons of God are partakers of the divine nature, having God's life, Spirit, and love within them, that the command is reasonable. For this reason, its obedience in ever-increasing measure is possible: Be perfect, as your Father is perfect. The perfection is our Father's. We have its seed in us; He delights to give the increase. The words that first appear to cast us down in utter helplessness now become our hope and strength. *"Be perfect, even as your Father...is perfect"* (Matthew 5:48). Claim your child's heritage; give yourself up to be wholly a son of God. Yield yourself to the Father to do in you all He is able to do.

And also remember who gives this message from the Father. It is the Son, who Himself was perfected through suffering by the Father. Jesus learned obedience, was made perfect, and has perfected us forever. The command *"Be perfect"* comes to us from Him, our elder Brother, as a promise of infinite hope. What Jesus asks of us, the Father gives. What Jesus speaks, He does. The aim of Christ and His gospel, is to *"present every man perfect in Christ Jesus"* (Colossians 1:28). Let us accept the command from Him. In yielding ourselves to Him, let us yield ourselves to obey His command.

Let our expectation be from Him in whom we have been perfected. Through faith in Him, we receive the Holy Spirit, by whom the love of God is shed abroad in our hearts. (See Romans 5:5.) Through faith in Him, that love becomes in us a fountain of love springing up into eternal life. (See John 4:14.) In union with Him, the love of God is perfected in us, and we are perfected in love. (See 1 John 4:18.) Let us not fear to accept and obey the command, *"Be perfect, even as your Father...is perfect."*

10

PERFECTED AS THE MASTER

Be ye therefore merciful, as your Father also is merciful....
The disciple is not above his master: but every one that is
perfect shall be as his master.
—Luke 6:36, 40

I n his report of part of the Sermon on the Mount, Luke records that Jesus does not say "Be perfect" but, *"Be ye therefore merciful, as your Father also is merciful"* (Luke 6:26). Then He introduces the word *perfect* immediately after; however, it is not mentioned in connection with the Father but in connection with the Son, as the Master of His disciples. The change is most instructive. It leads us to look to Jesus, as He dwelt in the flesh, as our model. It might be said that our circumstances and powers are so different from those of God that it is impossible to apply the standard of His infinite perfection in our little world. But here comes the Son, in the likeness of sinful flesh, tempted in all things as we are, and He offers Himself as our Master and Leader. He lives *with* us so that we may live *with* Him. He lives *like* us so that we may live *like* Him.

The divine standard is embodied and made visible, is brought within our reach, in the human model. As we grow into the likeness of Christ, who is the image of the Father, we will bear the likeness of the Father, too. Becoming like Him, the first-born among many brethren, we will become perfect as the Father is perfect. *"The disciple is not above his master: but every one that is perfect shall be as his master"* (Luke 6:40).

The thought of the disciple being as the Master sometimes involves outward humiliation. Like the Master, the disciple will be despised and persecuted. (See John 15:20.) And sometimes it refers to inward humility, the willingness to be a servant. (See Luke 22:27; John 13:16.) Both in his external life and in his inner disposition, the perfected disciple knows nothing higher than to be as his Master.

To take Jesus as one's Master, with the distinct desire and aim to be and live and act like Him—this is true Christianity. This is something far more than accepting Him as Savior and Helper. It is far more than even acknowledging Him as Lord and Master.

A servant may obey the commands of his master most faithfully, while he gives little thought to becoming like the master in likeness and spirit. This alone is full discipleship, to desire in everything to be as like the Master as much as possible and to count His life as the true expression of all that is perfect, aiming at nothing less than being perfect as He was. *"Every one that is perfect shall be as his master"* (Luke 6:40).

These words suggest to us that in discipleship there is more than one stage. In the Old Testament, it is only said of some that they served the Lord with a perfect heart, while it says of others that their hearts were not perfect with the Lord. (See 1 Kings 11:4, 15:3; 2 Chronicles 25:2.) Even so, there are still great differences between disciples today. There are some to whom the thought of aiming at the perfect likeness of the Master has never come. They only look to Christ as a Savior. And there are some people whose hearts indeed long for full conformity to their Lord, "to be as the Master," but who have never understood, though they have read the words, that there is such a thing as *a perfect heart* (2 Kings 20:3) and a life *"made perfect in love"* (1 John 4:18). But there are those to whom it has been given the ability to accept these words in their divine meaning and truth, and who do know in blessed experience what it is to say, along with Hezekiah, *"I have walked before thee in truth and with a perfect heart"* (2 Kings 20:3), and with John, *"As he is, so are we in this world"* (1 John 4:17).

As we go deeper in our study of what Scripture says of perfection, let us hold fast the principle we have learned here—the blessedness of likeness to Jesus in His humiliation and humility. The disciple's choice to take on the form of a servant, not exercising lordship and the need to be ministered to but instead girding himself to minister and to give his life for others—this is the secret of true perfection. *"The disciple is not above his master: but every one that is perfect shall be as his master"* (Luke 6:40). With the perfect love of God as our standard, with that love revealed in Christ's humanity and humility as our model and guide, with the Holy Spirit to strengthen us with might, that Christ may live in us, we will learn what this blessed verse means: *"Every one that is perfect shall be as his master."*

11

THE PERFECT FOLLOW CHRIST

Jesus said unto him, If thou wilt be perfect,
go and sell that thou hast, and give to the poor, and thou
shalt have treasure in heaven: and come and follow me.
—Matthew 19:21

For the rich young ruler, poverty was the path to perfection. *"The disciple is not above his master: but every one that is perfect shall be as his master"* (Luke 6:40). Poverty was part of the Master's perfection, part of that mysterious discipline of self-denial and suffering through which God desired to perfect Him. While on earth, poverty was to be the mark of all those who would always be with, and like, the Master.

What does this mean? Jesus was Lord of all. He might have lived here on earth in circumstances of comfort and with moderate possessions. He might have taught us how to own and to use and to sanctify property. He might in this have become like us, walking in the path in which most men have to walk. But He chose poverty. His life of self-sacrifice and direct dependence on God, His humiliation, and His trials and temptations were the elements of that highest perfection He exhibited.

Poverty was also to be the mark of the disciples' fellowship with the Father. It was to be the training school for perfect conformity to His image, the secret of power for victory over the world, for the full possession of the heavenly treasure, and for the full exhibition of the heavenly Spirit. And, even for Paul, who was called from the throne, poverty was the chosen and much-prized vehicle of his perfect fellowship with the Lord.

What does this mean? The command *"Be ye therefore perfect"* (Matthew 5:48) is for the rich as well as to the poor. Nowhere has Scripture spoken of the possession of property as a sin. While it warns against the danger riches bring and denounces their abuse, it has nowhere proposed a law forbidding riches. And yet it speaks of poverty as having a very high place in the life of perfection.

To understand this, we must remember that perfection is a relative term. We are not under a law, with its external commands of duty and conduct, which does not take into account diversity of character or circumstance. In the perfect law of liberty in which we are called to live, there is room for infinite variety in the manifestation of our devotion to God and Christ. According to the diversity of gifts and circumstances and callings, the same Spirit may be seen in apparently conflicting paths of life. There is a perfection which is sought in the right possession and use of earthly goods as the Master's steward. There is also a perfection which is sought even in external things to be as the Master Himself was and, in poverty, to bear witness to the reality and sufficiency of heavenly things.

In the early ages of the church, this truth that poverty is, for some, the path of perfection, exercised a mighty and a blessed influence. Men felt that poverty, as one of the traits of the holy life of Jesus and His apostles, was sacred and blessed. As the inner life of the church grew feeble, this spiritual truth was lost in external observances, and the fellowship of the poverty of Jesus was scarcely to be seen.

Poverty is a truth many are seeking after. If our Lord found poverty the best school for His own strengthening in the art of perfection and the surest way to rise above the world and win men's hearts for the Unseen, it should not surprise us if those we feel drawn to seek the closest possible conformity to their Lord even in material things. We should not be surprised that those who long for the highest possible power in witnessing for the Invisible should be irresistibly drawn to count this word as spoken to them, too: *"If thou wilt be perfect, go and sell that thou hast, and give to the poor, and thou shalt have treasure in heaven: and come and follow me"* (Matthew 19:21).

When this call is not felt, there is a larger lesson of universal application: There is no perfection without the sacrifice of all. To be perfected here on earth, Christ gave up all. To become like Him and to be perfected as the Master, we must give up all. The world and self must be renounced. For the Son said, *"If thou wilt be perfect, go and sell that thou hast, and give to the poor, and thou shalt have treasure in heaven: and come and follow me."*

12

THE PERFECT MAN

Howbeit we speak wisdom among them that are perfect.
—1 Corinthians 2:6

*And I, brethren, could not speak unto you as unto
spiritual, but as unto carnal, even as unto babes in
Christ....For ye are yet carnal: for whereas there is among
you envying, and strife, and divisions, are ye not carnal,
and walk as men?*
—1 Corinthians 3:1, 3

There were mighty and abundant operations of the Holy
Spirit among the Corinthians. Paul could say to them, *"In every
thing ye are enriched by him, in all utterance, and in all knowledge"*
(1 Corinthians 1:5). And yet in the sanctifying grace of the Holy
Spirit, there was much that was lacking. He had to say,

> *Now I beseech you, brethren, by the name of our Lord Jesus
> Christ...that there be no divisions among you; but that ye
> be perfectly joined together in the same mind and in the
> same judgment. For it hath been declared unto me of you...
> that there are contentions among you.*
> (1 Corinthians 1:10–11)

The spirit of humility and gentleness and unity was wanting. Without these they could not be perfected, either individually or as a body. They needed the injunction, *"And above all these things put on charity, which is the bond of perfectness"* (Colossians 3:14).

The Corinthians were as yet carnal. The gifts of the Spirit were among them in power, but they were very much lacking His grace—which renews, sweetens, and sanctifies every temper into the likeness of Jesus. The wisdom Paul preached was a heavenly, spiritual wisdom: *"But we speak the wisdom of God in a mystery, even the hidden wisdom"* (1 Corinthians 2:7). And they needed a spiritual, heavenly mind to understand it. *"We speak wisdom among them that are perfect"* (1 Corinthians 2:6). Paul said that he *"could not speak unto* [them] *as unto spiritual, but as unto carnal"* (1 Corinthians 3:1). Spiritual things must be spiritually discerned. The wisdom among the perfect could only be received by those who were spiritual, not carnal. The perfect ones of whom Paul speaks are the spiritual.

So who are the spiritual? The spiritual are those who have obtained supremacy and in whom is manifested the graces and gifts of the Spirit. God's love is His perfection. (See Matthew 5:40–46.) Christ's humility is His perfection. The self-sacrificing love of Christ, along with His humility, meekness, and gentleness, manifested in daily life, are the most perfect fruit of the Spirit. They are the true proof that a man is spiritual. A man may have great zeal in God's service—he may be used to influence many for good—and yet, when weighed in the balance of love, be may be found sadly wanting. It is in the heat of controversy or under unjust criticism that haste of temper, slowness to forgive and forget, or quick words and sharp judgments often reveal an easily wounded sensitiveness, which proves how little the Spirit of Christ has full possession or real mastery of a person. The spiritual man is the man who is clothed with the spirit of the suffering, crucified with Jesus.

And it is only the spiritual man who can understand the wisdom among the perfect.

> *Even the mystery which hath been hid from ages and from generations, but now is made manifest to his saints: To whom God would make known what is the riches of the glory of this mystery...which is Christ in you.*
>
> (Colossians 1:26–27)

A Christian teacher may be a man of wonderful perception and insight, and he may have the power of opening the truth, mightily stimulating it, and helping others, but yet have so much of the carnal that the deeper mystery of Christ in him remains hidden. It is only as we yield ourselves completely to the power of God's Holy Spirit that the Christian, whether scholar or teacher, can fully enter into the wisdom of the perfect. This yielding includes being set free from all that is carnal, attaining the utmost possible likeness to Jesus in His humiliation, and being filled with the Spirit who rules our hearts and lives.

To know the mind of God, we must have the mind of Christ. And the mind of Christ is this: He emptied and humbled Himself and became obedient to death. (See Philippians 2:8.) His humility was His capacity—His fitness—for rising to the throne of God. This humility must also be in us if the hidden wisdom of God is to be revealed to us in its power. It is this that is the mark of the spiritual man, the perfect man.

May God increase the number of the perfect ones. And to that end, may He increase the number of those who know to speak wisdom among the perfect, even God's wisdom. As the distinction between the carnal and the spiritual, the babes and the perfect, comes to recognition in the church, the connection between a spiritual life and a spiritual insight will become clearer. The call to perfection will gain new force and meaning. And it will once again be a just cause of reproof and of shame not to be among the perfect.

13

PERFECTING HOLINESS

Having therefore these promises, dearly beloved, let us cleanse ourselves from all filthiness of the flesh and spirit, perfecting holiness in the fear of God.
—2 Corinthians 7:1

These words give us an insight into one of the chief aspects of perfection and an answer to the question: In what are we to be perfect? We must be perfect in holiness. We must be perfectly holy. This is the explanation of the Father's message, *"Be ye therefore perfect"* (Matthew 5:48).

We know what holiness is. God alone is holy, and holiness is that which God communicates of Himself. Separation and cleansing and consecration are not holiness but only the preliminary steps on the way to it. The temple was holy because God dwelt in it. That which is given to God is not holy, but that which God accepts and appropriates, that which He takes possession of and takes up into His own fellowship and use—that is holy. *"Sanctify yourselves therefore, and be ye holy: for I am the LORD your God"* (Leviticus 20:7) was God's promise to His people of old, on which the command was based, *"Be ye therefore holy"* (Matthew 5:48). God's taking them for His own made them a holy people. Their entering into this holiness of God, yielding themselves to His will and fellowship and service, was what the command, "Be holy," called them to.

Even so, it is the same with us Christians. We are made holy in Christ; we are saints and holy ones. The call comes to us to follow after holiness, to perfect holiness, and to yield ourselves to the God who is ready to sanctify us wholly. It is the knowledge of what God has done in making us His holy ones, and has promised to do in sanctifying us wholly, that will give us courage to perfect holiness.

"Having therefore these promises, dearly beloved, let us...[perfect] *holiness in the fear of God"* (2 Corinthians 7:1). Which promises is this verse talking about? They are mentioned earlier on in the book: *"I will dwell in them...I will be their God"* (2 Corinthians 6:16); *"I will receive you and will be a Father unto you"* (verses 17–18). It was God's accepting the temple and dwelling there Himself that made it holy. It is God's dwelling in us that makes us holy and gives us not only the motivation but the courage and the power to perfect holiness—to yield ourselves to Him. It is God being a Father to us, begetting His own life, giving His own Son to us, forming Christ in us, until He makes His abode in us, that will give us confidence to believe that it is possible to perfect holiness. Then He will reveal to us the secret of its attainment. *"Having therefore these promises, dearly beloved"* (2 Corinthians 7:1), that is, knowing them, living by them, claiming them, and obtaining them—let us "perfect holiness."

This faith is the secret power of the growth of the inner life into perfect holiness. But there are hindrances which check and prevent this growth. These must be guarded against and removed. Every defilement, outward or inward, in conduct or sentiment, in the physical or the spiritual life, must be cleansed and cast away. Cleansing by the blood, cleansing by the Word, cleansing by the pruning-knife or the fire—in any way or by any means, we must be cleansed. In the fear of the Lord, every sin must be cut off and cast out; everything doubtful or defiling must be put away. Soul and body and spirit must be preserved entire and blameless. Thus cleansing ourselves from all defilement, we will perfect holiness. The spirit of holiness will fill God's temple with His holy presence and power.

Beloved, having these promises, let us perfect holiness. Perfectly holy! Perfect in holiness! Let us yield ourselves to these thoughts, to these wishes, to these promises of our God. Beginning with the perfect childlike heart, pressing on in the perfect way, clinging to a perfect Savior, living in fellowship with a God whose way and work is perfect, let us not be afraid to come to God with His own command as our prayer: Perfect holiness, O my Lord! He knows what He means by it, and we will also know if we follow on to know.

Let this be the spirit of our daily prayer. "Lord, I am called to perfect holiness. I come to You for it; make me as perfectly holy as a redeemed sinner can be on earth. I desire to walk before You with a perfect heart, perfect in Christ Jesus in the path of perfect holiness. I desire this day to come as near to perfection as grace can make it possible for me. 'Perfecting holiness' is, in the power of His Spirit, my goal.

14

BE PERFECT

This also we wish, even your perfection....
Finally, brethren, farewell. Be perfect, be of good comfort,
be of one mind, live in peace; and the God of love and
peace shall be with you.
—2 Corinthians 13:9, 11

The word *perfect* translated here means to bring a thing into its right condition, so that it is as it should be. It is used of mending nets, restoring them to their right state, or of equipping a ship, fitting it out with all it should have. It thus implies two things: the removal of all that is still wrong and the addition of all that is still lacking.

Within two verses, Paul uses the word *perfect* twice. He uses it first as the expression of the one thing which he asks of God for them, the summary of all grace and blessing. *"This also we wish, even your perfection"* (2 Corinthians 13:9). The wish is that they would be perfectly free from all that is wrong and carnal, and that they should perfectly possess and exhibit all that God would have them be.

Second, he uses it in a farewell word as the goal he would have them aim at. *"Finally, brethren, farewell. Be perfect"* (2 Corinthians 13:11). Then, three other verbs follow which show how this one, which takes the lead, relates to the Christian's daily life, showing what is to be his daily aim and experience. *"Be perfect, be of good comfort, be of one mind, live in peace"* (verse 11). Just as the comfort of the Spirit, the unity of love, and the life of peace are—if the God of love and peace is to be with us—our duty and our privilege every hour, so also is the goal of perfection. The close of the two epistles gathers up all its teaching in this one injunction: *"Farewell. Be perfect"* (verse 11).

The two texts together show us what the prayer and the preaching of every minister of the gospel ought to be. They show us what his heart, above everything, ought to be set on. With just cause, look on Paul as a model whom every minister ought to copy; let every gospel minister copy him in this, so that his people may know as he goes in and comes out that His heart breathes heavenward for them this one wish: Their perfection! Let each minister perform in such a way that his congregation may feel that all his teaching has this one aim: *"Be perfect"*!

If ministers are to seek this above everything in their charge of the church of God, they themselves need to feel deeply, and to expose faithfully, the low standard that prevails in the church. Some have said that they have seen perfectionism slay thousands. All must admit that imperfectionism has slain tens of thousands. Multitudes are soothing themselves in a life of worldliness and sin with the thought that as no one is perfect, imperfection cannot be so dangerous. Numbers of true Christians are making no progress because they have never known that we can serve God with a perfect heart—that the perfect heart is the secret of the perfect way, of a work going on to perfection. God's call to us to be perfect, to perfect holiness in reverence to Him, to live perfect in Christ Jesus, to stand perfect in all the will of God, must be preached. It must be preached until faith begins to live again in the church and that all teaching is summed up in the words, *"Be perfect."* Each day of our life needs to be spent under their inspiration.

When ministers know themselves and are known as the messengers of this God-willed perfection, they will feel the need of nothing less than the teaching of the Holy Spirit to guide men in this path. They will see and preach that religion must indeed be a surrender of all to God. It is truly becoming as conformed to His will, living as entirely to His glory, being as perfectly devoted to His service, as grace can enable us to be. And no less! This conformity will be the only rule of duty and measure of expectation.

The message *"Be perfect"* will demand the whole heart, the whole life, the whole strength. As the soul learns each day to say, "Father, I will be perfect in heart with You, this day. I will walk before You and be perfect," the need and the meaning of abiding in Christ will be better understood. Christ Himself with His power and love will have new preciousness, and God will prove what He can do for our souls, for a church wholly given up to Him.

O ministers of Christ, you messengers of His salvation, say to the churches over which the Holy Spirit has made you overseers: *"This also we wish, even your perfection....Finally, brethren....Be perfect"*!

15

NOT PERFECTED, YET PERFECT

*Not as though I had already attained, either were already
perfect: but I follow after....One thing I do, forgetting those
things which are behind, and reaching forth unto those
things which are before, I press toward the mark....Let us
therefore, as many as be perfect, be thus minded.*
—Philippians 3:12–15

There are degrees of perfection. We have perfect, more perfect, and most perfect. We have perfect, and waiting to be perfected. So it was with our Lord Jesus. In Hebrews, we read three times of Him that He was perfected or made perfect. There was not the faintest shadow of sinful imperfection in Him. At each moment of His life, He was perfect—just what He should be. And yet He needed it, and it suited God to perfect Him through suffering and the obedience He learned in it. As He conquered temptation, maintained His allegiance to God, and, amid heartfelt crying and tears, gave up His will to God's will, His human nature was perfected, and He became a High Priest, the *"Son, perfected for evermore"* (Hebrews 7:28 asv). During His life on earth, Jesus was perfect but yet not perfected.

"The disciple...that is perfect shall be as his master" (Luke 6:40). What is true of Him is true, in measure, of us, too. Paul wrote to the Corinthians of speaking wisdom among the perfect, a wisdom carnal Christians could not understand. Here in our text, he classes himself with the perfect and expects and enjoins them to be of the same mind with himself. He sees no difficulty either in speaking of himself and others as perfect, or in regarding the perfect as needing to be yet fully perfected.

And now what is this perfection which has yet to be perfected? And who are these perfect ones? The man who has made the highest perfection his choice, and who has given his whole heart and life to attain it, is counted by God a perfect man: *"The kingdom of heaven is like to a grain of mustard seed"* (Matthew 13:31). Where God sees in the heart the single purpose to be all that God wills, He sees the divine seed of all perfection. And as He counts faith for righteousness, so He counts this whole-hearted purpose to be perfect as the beginning of perfection. The man with a perfect heart is accepted by God, even amid all imperfection of attainment, as a perfect man. Paul could look upon the church and unhesitatingly say, *"As many as be perfect, be thus minded"* (Philippians 3:15).

We know how he describes two classes among the Corinthians. The one, the large majority, was carnal and content to live in strife; the other, the spiritual, was perfect. In the church of our day, it is to be feared that the great majority of believers have no conception of their calling to be perfect. They do not have the slightest idea that it is their duty not only to be Christian, but to be as eminently spiritual, as full of grace and holiness, as it is possible for God to make them. Even where there is some measure of earnest purpose in the pursuit of holiness, there is such a lack of faith in the earnestness of God's purpose when He speaks *"Be perfect,"* and in the sufficiency of His grace to meet the demand, that the appeal meets no response. In no real sense do they understand or accept Paul's invitation: *"Let us therefore, as many as be perfect, be thus minded"* (Philippians 3:15).

But, thank God! It is not so with all. There is an ever-increasing number who cannot forget that God means what He says when He speaks, *"Be perfect,"* and who regard themselves as under the most solemn obligation to obey the command. These words of Christ are to them a revelation of what Christ is come to give and to work, a promise of the blessing to which His teaching and leading will bring them. They have joined the band of like-minded ones who Paul would associate himself with. They seek God with their whole heart. They serve Him with a perfect heart. Their one aim in life is to be made perfect, even as the Master.

My reader, we are in the presence of God, who has said to you: *"Be perfect"*! We are in the presence of Christ Jesus, who gave Himself that you might obey this command of your God. Here I charge you, do not refuse the call of God's servant but enroll yourself among those who accept it. Do not fear to take your place before God with Paul among the perfect in heart. It will be so far from causing self-complacency that you will learn from Him how the perfect have yet to be perfected, and how the one mark of the perfect is that they count all things loss as they press on to the mark of the high calling of God in Jesus Christ. (See Philippians 3:14.)

16

PERFECT, YET TO BE PERFECTED

Not as though I had already attained, either were already
perfect...one thing I do, forgetting those things which are
behind, and reaching forth unto those things which are
before, I press toward the mark....Let us therefore,
as many as be perfect, be thus minded....
Brethren, be followers together of me.
—Philippians 3:12–15, 17

The mark of the perfect, as demonstrated by Paul and all who are thus minded, is the passionate desire to be yet made perfect. This seems like a paradox. And yet what we see in our Master proves the truth of what we say. The consciousness of being perfect is in entire harmony with the readiness to sacrifice life itself for the sake of being yet made perfect. It was thus with Christ. It was thus with Paul. It will be thus with us, as we open our hearts fully and give God's words room and time to do their work.

Many think that the more imperfect one is, the more he will feel his need of perfection. All experience, in every department of life, teaches us the very opposite. It is those who are nearest perfection who most know their need of being perfected.

They are the ones most ready to make any sacrifice to attain to it. To count everything loss for perfection in practice is the surest proof that perfection in principle has possession of the heart. The more honestly and earnestly the believer claims that he seeks God with a perfect heart, the more ready he will be to say with Paul: *"Not as though I had already attained, either were already perfect"* (Philippians 3:12).

In what did Paul long to be made perfect? Read the wonderful passage with care—without prejudice or preconceived ideas—and I think you will see that He gives here no indication of it being sin or sinful imperfection from which he was seeking to be perfectly free. Whatever his writings teach elsewhere, the thought is not in his mind here. The perfected disciple is as his Master. Paul is speaking here of his life and lifework, and He feels that it will not be perfected until he has reached the goal and obtained the prize. To this he is pressing on. He who runs in a race may, as far as he has gone, have done everything perfectly. All may pronounce his course perfect as far as it has gone. Still, it has to be perfected. The prize has to be won. The contrast is not with failure or shortcoming but with what is as yet unfinished and waiting for its full end. And so Paul uses expressions which tell us that what he already had of Christ was but a part. He did know Christ; he had gained Christ; he was found in Him; he had understood in wonderful measure that for which Christ had apprehended him. And yet all these things—knowing Christ, gaining Him, being found in Him, understanding that for which he was apprehended—he speaks of as being what he was striving after with all his might: *"If by any means I might attain unto the resurrection of the dead...I press toward the mark for the prize"* (Philippians 3:11, 14). It is of all this he says, *"Not as though I had already attained, either were already perfect...Let us therefore, as many as be perfect, be thus minded"* (verses 12, 15).

Paul had known Christ for many years, but he still knew there were in Him riches and treasures greater than he had yet known. Nothing could satisfy him but the full and final eternal possession of what the resurrection could bring him. For this he counted all things but loss; for this he forgot the things that were behind; for this he pressed toward the mark, unto the prize. He teaches us the spirit of true perfection. A man who knows he is perfect with God—a man who knows he must yet be perfected, a man who knows that he has counted all things loss to attain this final perfection—such is the perfect man.

Christian, learn here the price of perfection, as well as the mark of the perfect ones. The Master gave His life to be made perfect forever. Paul did the same. It is a solemn thing to profess the pursuit of perfection. The price of a pearl of great value is high: all things must be counted as loss. I have urged you to put your names on the class list of the perfect—to ask the Master to put it down and give you the blessed witness of the Spirit to a perfect heart. I urge you now, if, like Paul, you claim to be perfect, single and wholehearted in your surrender to God, live the life of the perfect—with the verse *"count all things but loss"* (Philippians 3:8) as your watchword. May your one desire be to possess Him wholly, to be possessed of Him, and to be made perfect, even as He was.

O Father, be pleased to open the eyes of Your children, that they may see what the perfection of heart is that You now ask of them, and what the perfection in Christ is that You would have them seek at any cost.

17

PERFECT IN CHRIST

To whom God would make known what is the riches of the glory of this mystery among the Gentiles; which is Christ in you, the hope of glory: Whom we preach, warning every man, and teaching every man in all wisdom; that we may present every man perfect in Christ Jesus: Whereunto I also labour, striving according to his working, which worketh in me mightily.
—Colossians 1:27–29

*P*erfect in Christ Jesus" (Colossians 1:28). While searching the Word regarding perfection, we have here a new word opening up to us the hope—the assurance—of what is our duty. It links all that we have seen of God's call and claim with all that we know of Christ in His grace and power. *"Perfect in Christ Jesus."* Here is the open gateway into the perfect life. He who is given clear insight into what this means finds through it an entrance into the life of Christian perfectness.

There are three aspects in which we need to look at the truth of our being perfect in Christ. There is, first, our perfection in Christ, *as it is prepared for us in Him our Head.* As the second Adam, Christ came and brought about a new nature for all the members of His body. This nature is His own life, perfected through suffering and obedience. In thus being perfected Himself, He forever perfected those who are sanctified. His perfection, His perfect life, is ours. And it is ours not only judicially, or by imputation, but it is an actual spiritual reality, in virtue of our real and living union with Him. Paul says in the same epistle, *"In him dwelleth all the fulness of the Godhead bodily. And ye are complete in him"* (Colossians 2:9–10). All that you are to be is already fulfilled, and so you are fulfilled in Him. You are circumcised in Him, buried with Him, raised with Him, and quickened together with Him. All of Christ's members are in Him, fulfilled in Him.

Then, second, there is our perfection in Christ, *as imparted to us by the Holy Spirit in uniting us to Him.* The life which is implanted in us at the new birth—planted into the midst of a mass of sin and flesh—is a perfect life. As the seed contains in itself the whole life of the tree, so the seed of God within us is the perfect life of Christ, with its power to grow and to fill our life and to bring forth fruit to perfection.

And then, third, there is also our perfection in Christ, *as brought about in us by the Holy Spirit, appropriated by us in the obedience of faith, and made manifest in our life and conduct.* Our faith grasps and feeds upon the truth in the two former aspects and yields itself to God to have that perfect life master and pervade the whole of our daily lives in its ordinary actions. Then, *"perfect in Christ Jesus"* will become each moment a practical reality and experience. All that the Word has taught of the perfect heart and the perfect way—of being perfect as the Father and perfect as the Master—shines with new meaning and with the light of a new life. Christ, the living Christ, is our Perfection. He Himself lives each day and hour to impart it. The measureless love of Jesus, and the power of the endless life in which His life works, become the measure of our expectation. In the life we now live in the flesh, with its daily duties in dealing with men and money, with care and temptation, we are to demonstrate that perfect in Christ is no mere ideal, but that it is, in the power of Almighty God, simple and literal truth.

It is in the last of these three aspects that Paul has used the expression in our text. He speaks of admonishing every man, and teaching every man, in all wisdom, that he may present every man perfect in Christ Jesus. The admonishing and teaching refer to the perfection in daily life and walk. In principle, Christians are perfect in Christ. In practice, they are to become perfect. The aim of the gospel ministry among believers is to present every man perfect in Christ Jesus—to teach men how they might put on the Lord Jesus, have His life cover them, and have His life in them.

What a task! What a hopeless task to the minister, as he looks upon the state of the church! But what a task of infinite hopefulness if he does his work as Paul did, striving for nothing less than presenting every man perfect in Christ. *"Christ in you, the hope of glory: whom we preach, warning every man, and teaching every man in all wisdom; that we may present every man perfect in Christ Jesus"* (Colossians 1:28–29). The aim is high, but the power is divine. Let the minister, in full purpose of heart, make Paul's aim his own: to present every man perfect in Christ Jesus. He may count upon the same strength Paul had: *"[Christ's] working, which worketh in me mightily"* (verse 29).

18

PERFECT IN GOD'S WILL

Epaphras, who is one of you, a servant of Christ, saluteth you, always labouring fervently for you in prayers, that ye may stand perfect and complete in all the will of God.
—Colossians 4:12

In this epistle, as in others, the life of the believer as he lives it in heaven in Christ, and then as he lives it here on earth with men, is set before us. The teaching of Scripture is intensely spiritual and supernatural, but, at the same time, it is intensely human and practical. This comes out very beautifully in the two expressions above. Paul had told the Colossians what he labored for. He now tells them what another minister, Epaphras, asked on their behalf. Paul's striving was in his labor that they might be *"perfect in Christ Jesus"* (Colossians 1:28). The striving of Epaphras was in the prayer that they might be *"perfect and complete in all the will of God."*

First we have *"perfect in Christ Jesus."* The thought is so unearthly and divine that its full meaning eludes our grasp. It lifts us up to live in Christ and heaven. Then we have *"perfect and complete in all the will of God."* This word brings us down to earth and daily life. It places all under the rule of God's will and calls us in every action and disposition to live in the will of God.

The perfection of the creature consists in nothing but willing the will of the Creator. The will of God is the expression of the divine perfection. Nature has its beauty and glory in being the expression of divine will. The angels have their place and bliss in heaven in doing God's will. The Son of God was perfected in learning obedience, in giving Himself up to the will of God. His redemption has but one object: to bring man into the only place of rest and blessedness—the will of God. The prayer of Epaphras shows how truly he had entered into the spirit of his Master. He prays for His people, that they may stand in the will of God, in *all* the will of God—nothing in their life excepted. He prays that they may be perfect in all the will of God at each moment, walking in a perfect way. Perfect in all the will of God is his one thought of what ought to be asked, and could be found, in prayer.

Paul prayed for the Colossians, *"that* [they] *might be filled with the knowledge of his will in all wisdom and spiritual understanding"* (Colossians 1:9). Paul and Epaphras were two servants of God but of one mind. They both believed that converts must be reminded that their knowledge of God's will is defective, that they need to pray for a divine teaching to know that will, and that their one aim should be to stand perfect in all that will.

Let all seekers after perfection—all who would be like-minded with Paul—note well the lesson. In the joy of consecration sealed by the Holy Spirit, in the consciousness of a whole-hearted purpose, and in service to God with a perfect heart, the believer is often tempted to forget how much of God's will he does not yet see. There may be grave defects in his character, serious shortcomings from the law of perfect love in his conduct, which others can observe. The consciousness of acting up to the full light of what we know to be right is a most blessed thing, one of the marks of the perfect heart. But it must always be accompanied by the remembrance of how much there may be that has not yet been revealed to us.

This sense of ignorance as to much of God's will—this conviction that there is still much in us that needs to be changed, sanctified, and perfected—will make us very humble and tender, very watchful and hopeful in prayer. Far from interfering with our consciousness that we serve God with a perfect heart, it will give it new strength, while it cultivates that humility which is the greatest beauty of perfection. Without it, the appeal to the consciousness of our uprightness becomes superficial and dangerous, and the doctrine of perfection a stumbling block and a snare.

"Perfect and complete in all the will of God." Let this be our unceasing aim and prayer. Let it strike its roots deep in the humility which comes from the conviction of how much there is yet to be revealed to us. And let it be strengthened by the consciousness that we have given ourselves to serve Him with a perfect heart, full of the glad purpose to be content with nothing less than standing perfect in all the will of God. We can rejoice in the confidence of what God will do for those who are before Him perfect in Christ Jesus. Let our faith claim the full blessing. God will reveal to us how *"perfect in Christ Jesus"* and *"perfect and complete in all the will of God"* are one in His thought, and may even be so in our experience.

Paul prayed for the Colossians without ceasing, that they might be filled with the knowledge of God's will. Epaphras was *"always labouring fervently for* [them] *in prayers"* (Colossians 4:12), that they might stand perfect in all the will of God. It is by prayer, by unceasing striving in prayer, that this grace must be sought for the church. It is before the throne, in the presence of God, that the life of perfection must be found and lived. It is by the operation of the mighty quickening power of God Himself—waited for and received in prayer—that believers can indeed stand perfect in all the will of God. God give us grace to seek and to find.

19

CHRIST MADE PERFECT

For it became him...to make the captain of their salvation
perfect through sufferings.
—Hebrews 2:10

Though he were a Son, yet learned he obedience
by the things which he suffered;
and being made perfect, he became the author of
eternal salvation unto all them that obey him.
—Hebrews 5:8–9

But the word of the oath, which was after the law,
appointeth a Son, perfected for evermore.
—Hebrews 7:28 (asv)

Here we have three passages in which we are taught that Jesus Christ Himself, though He was the Son of God, had to be perfected. The first tells us that it was as the captain of our salvation that He was perfected. It was God's work to perfect Him. There was a need for it: *"It became* [God]*"* (Hebrews 2:10) to do it. It was through suffering that work was accomplished. The second tells us what the power of suffering was to perfection. In it, He learned obedience to God's will, and being thus perfected, He became the author of eternal salvation to all who obey Him. The third tells us that it is as the *"Son, perfected for evermore"* (Hebrews 7:28 ASV) that He is appointed High Priest in the heavens.

The words open to us the innermost secret of Christian perfection. The Christian has no other perfection than the perfection of Christ. The deeper his insight into the character of his Lord, as having been made perfect by being brought into perfect union with God's will through suffering and obedience, the more clearly he will understand what that redemption which Christ came to bring really consists of and what the path to its full enjoyment truly is.

There was nothing of sinful defect or shortcoming in Christ. He was from His birth the perfect One. And yet He needed to be perfected. There was that in His human nature which needed to grow, to be strengthened and developed, and which could only thus be perfected. He had to follow on, and, step-by-step, the will of God opened up to Him. In the midst of temptation and suffering, He had to learn and prove what it was to do that will alone at any cost. It is *this* Christ who is our Leader and Forerunner, our High Priest and Redeemer. And it is as this perfection of His—this being made perfect through obedience to God's will—is revealed to us, that we will know fully what the redemption is that He brings.

We learn to take Him as our example. Like Him we say, *"I am come, not to do my own will, but the will of Him that sent me"* (John 6:38). We accept the will of God as the one thing we have to live for and to live in. In every circumstance and trial, we see and bow to the will of God. We meet every providential appointment in every ordinary duty of daily life as God's will. We pray to be filled with the knowledge of His will, that we may enter into it in its fullness, that we may stand complete in all the will of God. Whether we suffer or obey God's will, we seek to be perfected as the Master was.

We not only take Christ as our example and law in the path of perfection but as the promise and pledge of what we are to be. All that Christ was and did as Intercessor, Representative, Head, and Savior, is for us. All He does is in the power of the endless life. This perfection of His is the perfection of His life, His way of living. This life of His, perfected in obedience, is now ours. He gives us His own Spirit to breathe and to work it in us. He is the Vine; we are the branches. The very mind and disposition that was in Him on earth is communicated to us.

Yet there is even more—it is not only Christ in heaven who imparts to us something of His Spirit; Christ Himself comes to dwell in our heart—the Christ who was made perfect through learning obedience. It is in this character that He reigns in heaven. "[He] *became obedient unto death, even the death of the cross. Wherefore God also hath highly exalted him*" (Philippians 2:8–9). It is in this character that He dwells and rules in the heart! The real character, the essential attribute of the life Christ lived on earth, and which He maintains in us, is this: a will that is perfect with God. It is a will that is ready, at any cost, to be perfected in all of *His* will. It is this character He imparts to His own: the perfection with which He was perfected in learning obedience. As those who are perfect in Christ, who are perfect of heart toward God and are pressing on to be made perfect, may they live in the will of God. Let our one desire be to be even as He was, to do God's will, and to stand perfect in all the will of God.

20

GO ON TO PERFECTION

But strong meat belongeth to them that are of full age, even those who by reason of use have their senses exercised to discern both good and evil.
—Hebrews 5:14

Therefore leaving the principles of the doctrine of Christ, let us go on unto perfection.
—Hebrews 6:1

The writer had reproved the Hebrews for being slow to hear; for having made no progress in the Christian life; and for still being as little children who needed milk. They could not bear solid food—the deeper and more spiritual teaching in regard to the heavenly state of life into which Christ had entered—the life into which He admits those who are ready for it. The writer calls those who are ready the perfect, mature, or full-grown men of the house of God. We must not associate the ideas of mature and full-grown with time. In the Christian life, it is not as it is in nature. A believer of three years may be counted among the mature or perfect. One of twenty years may be but a babe, unskilled in the Word of righteousness. Nor must we associate it with power of intellect or maturity of judgment. These may be found without that insight into spiritual truth and that longing after the highest attainable perfection in character and fellowship with God, of which Paul is speaking.

We are told what the distinguishing characteristics are of the perfect one: *"Those who by reason of use have their senses exercised to discern both good and evil"* (Hebrews 5:14). It is the desire after holiness, the tender conscience that longs above everything to discern good and evil, the heart that seeks only and always and fully to know and do the will of God that marks the perfect man. He who has set his heart upon being holy and, in the pursuit after the highest moral and spiritual perfection, exercises his senses in everything to discern good and evil, is counted the perfect man.

This epistle has spoken of the two stages of the Christian life. It now calls upon the Hebrews to no longer be babes, to no longer remain content with the first principles—the basic elements of the doctrine of Christ. With the exhortation, *"Let us go on unto perfection"* (Hebrews 6:1), the author invites his hearers to come and learn how Jesus is a Priest with the power of an endless life, who can save completely. It urges them to know how He is the Mediator of a better covenant, lifting us into a better life by writing the law in our heart. It presses them to discover how the Holiest of all has been set open for us to enter in and is there to serve the living God. *"Let us go on unto perfection"* is the waymark pointing all to that heavenly life in God's presence, which can be lived even here on earth. This is what the full knowledge of Jesus as our heavenly High Priest leads us to.

This is not the first time we see the word *perfection* in this epistle. We read of God's perfecting of Christ through suffering.

Perfection is that perfect union between us and God's will, that blessed meekness and surrender to God's will that the Father worked in Christ through suffering. We read of Christ's learning obedience and His being made perfect. This is the true maturity or perfection, the true wisdom among the perfect—the knowing and the doing of God's will. We read of strong food for the perfect, who, by reason of use, have their senses exercised to discern both good and evil. Here again perfection is, even as with Christ, the disposition—the character—that is formed when a man is conformed to God's will. This conformity is fellowship with God in His holiness—the one aim of His life, to which everything else, even life itself, is to be sacrificed.

Jesus our High Priest, and the further teaching of this epistle, would lead us to this. The knowledge of the mysteries of God, of the highest spiritual truth, cannot profit us; we have no inward capacity for receiving them, unless our inmost life is yielded to receive the perfection by which Jesus was perfected as our own. When we find this quality, the Holy Spirit then reveals to us how Christ, in the power of an endless life, has forever perfected those who are sanctified. He has prepared a life, a disposition, with which He clothes them. And we will understand that *"Let us go on unto perfection"* means just this, "Let us go on to know Christ perfectly—to live entirely by His heavenly life." Now that He is perfected, we are to wholly follow His earthly life and the path in which He reached perfection. Union with Christ in heaven will mean likeness to Christ on earth in His lamblike meekness and humility, in that Sonlike obedience through which He entered glory. Brethren, leaving the first principles, let us go on to perfection.

21

NO PERFECTION BY
THE LAW

*If therefore perfection were by the Levitical priesthood, (for
under it the people received the law,) what further need
was there that another priest should rise after the order of
Melchisedec....Who is made, not after the law of a carnal
commandment, but after the power of an endless life....
For there is verily a disannulling of the commandment
going before for the weakness and unprofitableness thereof.
For the law made nothing perfect.*
—Hebrews 7:11, 16, 18–19

*Which were offered both gifts and sacrifices,
that could not make him that did the service perfect,
as pertaining to the conscience.*
—Hebrews 9:9

*For the law having a shadow of good things to come...can
never...make the comers thereunto perfect.*
—Hebrews 10:1

*God having provided some better thing for us, that they
without us should not be made perfect.*
—Hebrews 11:40

Of the Epistles of the New Testament, there are none in which the word *perfect* is used so often as that to the Hebrews. And there are no epistles that will help us to better see what Christian perfection is, and the way to its attainment, than this epistle. *Perfect* is used three times of our Lord Jesus and His being made perfect Himself. Twice it is used of our perfection. Five times it mentions the perfection of which the law was the shadow, but which could not be till Jesus came. Three times it speaks of Christ's work in perfecting us, and once of the work of God in perfecting us. These five distinct thoughts each give us a subject of meditation. We have already spoken of the first two. We need to uncover the other three areas.

A careful examination of the verses above will show that the writer thought it important enough to make it clear that the law could perfect no person or thing. It was vital to stress this, both because of the close connection in which the law stood to the true perfection, as its promise and preparation, and because of the natural tendency of the human heart to seek perfection by the law. It was not only the Hebrews who greatly needed this teaching. Among Christians in our days, the greatest hindrance in accepting the perfection the gospel asks of us and offers to us is that they make the law their standard. Then they make their inability to fulfill the law the excuse for not attaining it and for not even seeking it. They have never understood that the law is only a preparation for something better, that when that which is perfect is come, that which is in part is done away.

The law demands; the law calls for effort. The law demands that each self does its utmost. But it makes nothing perfect, neither the conscience nor the worshipper. This is what Christ came to bring. The very perfection which the law could not give,

He gives. The epistle tells us that He was made a Priest (not as Aaron, after the law and in connection with the service of a carnal commandment, which had to be disannulled because of its weakness and unprofitableness, but after the power of an endless life). What Christ, as Priest, has worked and now works, is all in the power of an inward birth, a new life, and eternal life. What is born unto me—what is as spirit and life within me—has its own power of growth and action. Christ's being made perfect Himself through suffering and obedience—His having perfected us by that same sacrifice—and His communication of that perfection to us is all in the power of an endless life. It works in us as a life power; in no other way could we become partakers of it.

Perfection does not come through the law; let us listen to the blessed lesson. Let us take the warning. The law is so closely connected with perfection—was so long its only representative and forerunner—that we can hardly realize that it makes nothing perfect. Let us heed the encouragement: What the law could not do, God, in sending His Son, has done. (See Hebrews 10:1.) The Son, perfected forevermore, has perfected us forever. It is in Jesus we have our perfection. It is in living union with Him, when He is within us, not only as a seed or a little child but formed within us and dwelling within us, that we will know how much He can make us perfect. It is faith that leads us in the path toward perfection. It is faith that sees, receives, lives in Jesus the perfect One, and it is what will lead us on to the perfection God would have.

22

CHRIST PERFECTED US

But Christ being come an high priest of good things to come, by a greater and more perfect tabernacle,...entered in once into the holy place.
—Hebrews 9:11–12

By one offering he hath perfected for ever them that are sanctified.
—Hebrews 10:14

In Christ's work, as set before us in the epistle to the Hebrews, there are two parts. In contrast with the worldly sanctuary, He is the minister of the true tabernacle. The holiest One of all is now open to us. Christ has opened the way through a more perfect tabernacle into the presence of God. He has prepared and opened up for us a place of perfect fellowship with God and, in a life of faith (which means a life in full union with Christ), a place of access into God's immediate presence. There must be harmony between the place of worship and the worshipper. As He has prepared the perfect sanctuary—the Holiest of all for us— He has prepared us for it, too. *"By one offering he hath perfected for ever them that are sanctified.*" For the sanctuary, there are sanctified ones; for the holiest One of all, a holy priesthood; for the perfect tabernacle, the perfected worshipper.

"*By one offering he hath perfected for ever them that are sanctified.*" The word "*perfected*" here cannot mean anything different from what it meant in the three passages where it has been previously used of Him, namely, in Hebrews 2:11, 5:9, and 7:28. They all point to that which constitutes the real value, the innermost nature, of His sacrifice. He was Himself perfected for our sake, that He might perfect us with the same perfection God had perfected Him with. What is this perfection with which God perfected Christ through suffering, in which Christ was perfected through obedience, in which the Son, perfected forevermore, was made our High Priest?

The answer is to be found in what the object of Christ's redeeming work was and still is. The perfection of man at creation consisted in this: that he had a will with power to will as God willed, and so to enter into inner union with the divine life of holiness and glory. Man's fall was a turning from the will of God to do the will of self. And so this self and self-will became the source and the curse of sin. The work of Christ was to bring men back to that will of God, which alone is life and blessedness. Therefore, God made Him perfect through suffering. This was proper and needful if He was to be the Leader of our salvation. In His own person, He was to conquer sin. He was to develop and bring to perfection a real human life, sacrificing everything that men hold dear—willing to give up even life itself in surrender to God's will—and proving that it is the meat, the very life of man's spirit, to do God's will.

This was the perfection with which Christ was perfected as our High Priest, who brings us back to God. This was the meaning and the value of His sacrifice, that *"one offering"* by which *"he hath perfected for ever them that are sanctified."* In the same sacrifice in which He was perfected, He perfected us. As the second Adam, He made us partakers of His own perfection. Just as Adam in his death corrupted us and our nature forevermore, so Christ in His death, in which He Himself was perfected, perfected us and our nature forevermore. He has brought about a new, perfect nature for us, a new life. With Him we died unto sin; in Him we live unto God.

And how do we become partakers of this perfection with which Christ has perfected us? First of all, the conscience is perfected so that we have no more conscience of sin and enter boldly into the holiest place of all, the presence of God. The consciousness of a perfect redemption possesses and fills the soul. And then, as we abide in this, God Himself perfects us to do His will in every good thing, working in us that which is pleasing in His sight, through Jesus Christ. Through Christ—the High Priest in the power of the endless life—there comes to us in a constant stream from on high, the power of the heavenly life, so that day by day we may present ourselves perfect in Christ Jesus.

Truly there are Christians who seek to dwell in the divine perfection which the epistle to the Hebrews speaks of. These believers hold fellowship with Him who, in such intense human reality, was perfected through suffering and obedience. They turn in faith to Him who has perfected us. They look to Him to communicate His perfection to us each day as we practice walking in His footsteps. These believers may most surely count that He Himself will lead them into the promised inheritance of perfection.

23

GOD PERFECTED YOU

Now the God of peace, that brought again from the dead our Lord Jesus, that great shepherd of the sheep, through the blood of the everlasting covenant, make you perfect in every good work to do his will, working in you that which is wellpleasing in his sight, through Jesus Christ; to whom be glory for ever and ever. Amen.
—Hebrews 13:20–21

These two verses summarize the whole epistle to the Hebrews in the form of a prayer. In the first verse, we have the substance of what was taught in the first half of the epistle—what God has done for us in the redemption in Christ Jesus. In the second verse, we have a revelation and a promise of what the God of redemption will do for us. Here we see how God's one aim and desire is to make us perfect. We have said before, the word *perfect* here implies the removal of all that is wrong and the supply of all that is wanting. This is what God wants to do in us. *"Our Lord Jesus…make[s] you perfect in every good work."*

We need a large faith to claim this promise. So that our faith may be full and strong, we are reminded of what God has already done for us. This is the assurance of what He will yet do in us. Let us look to Him as the God of peace, who has made peace in the entire putting away of sin, who now proclaims peace, and who gives perfect peace. Let us look to Jesus Christ, the Great Shepherd of the sheep, our High Priest and King, who loves to care for us and keep us. Let us remember the blood of the everlasting covenant and the power by which God raised Christ from the dead and allowed Him to enter into heaven. That blood is God's pledge that the covenant, with its promises, will be fulfilled in our hearts. Let us think of God's raising Him from the dead, that our faith and hope might be in God. The power that raised Jesus is the power that works in us. Yes, let us look and worship and adore this God of peace, who has done it all, who raised Christ through the blood of the covenant, that we might know and trust Him.

And let us believe the message that tells us that this God of peace will perfect you in every good work. The God who perfected Christ will perfect you, too. The God who has worked out such a perfect salvation for us will perfect it in us. The more we gaze upon Him who has done such wondrous things for us, the more we will trust Him for this wondrous thing He promises to do in us: to perfect us in every good thing. What God did in Christ is the measure of what He will do in us to make us perfect. The same Omnipotence that worked in Christ to perfect Him waits for our faith to trust Him working in us day by day to perfect us in the doing of God's will. And the surrender to be made perfect will be the measure of our capacity to understand what God has done in Christ.

And now hear what this perfection is which God promises to work in us. It is truly divine, as divine as the work of redemption: *"The God of peace, that brought again from the dead our Lord Jesus"* (Hebrews 13:20) perfects you. It is intensely practical: *"In every good work to do his will"* (verse 21). It is universal, with nothing excluded from its operation: *"In every good work"* (Hebrews 13:21). It is truly human and personal: God perfects us, so that we do His will. It is inward: God working *in us* that which is pleasing in His sight. And it is most blessed, giving us the consciousness that our life pleases Him, because it is His own work we do: He works in us *"that which is wellpleasing in his sight"* (verse 21).

"[God making] you perfect in every good work to do his will" (verse 21) is the conclusion of the whole epistle. *"To do his will"* (verse 21) is the blessedness of the angels in heaven. For this the Son became man; by this He was perfected; in this *"we are sanctified"* (Hebrews 10:10). It is *"to do his will"* (Hebrews 13:21) that God perfects us, that God works in us that which is pleasing in His sight.

Believer, let God's aim be yours. Say to God that you do desire this above everything. Give yourself at once entirely, absolutely, to this, and say with the Son, *"Lo, I come to do thy will, O God"* (Hebrews 10:9). This will give you an insight into the meaning, the need, and the preciousness of the promise, *"[God] make you perfect in every good work to do his will."* This will fix your heart upon God in the wondrous light of the truth. He who perfected Christ is perfecting me, too. This will give you confidence, in the fullness of faith, to claim this God as your God, the God who perfects you in every good work.

The perfecting of the believer by God—restoring him to his right condition to fit him for doing His will—may be instantaneous. A valuable piece of machinery may be out of order. The owner spends time and trouble in vain to put it right. Then the maker comes, and it takes him but a moment to see and remove the hindrance. And so the soul that has for years wearied itself in the effort to do God's will, may often in one moment be delivered from some misunderstanding as to what God demands or promises, and then it finds itself restored, perfected for every good work. And what was done in a moment becomes the secret of the continuous life, as faith each day yields to the God that perfects, to do that which is well-pleasing in His sight.

Yes, the soul that dares say to God that it yields itself in everything to do His will—and through all the humiliation which comes from the sense of emptiness and weakness, abides by its vow in simple trust—will be made strong to rise, to appropriate, and to experience in full measure what God has offered in His precious Word. The God of peace perfect you in every good work to do His will, working in you that which is pleasing in His sight, through Jesus Christ.

And the soul will sing with new meaning, and in fullness of joy, it will sing the song of adoring love: To Him be glory forever and ever. Amen.

24

PERFECT PATIENCE

But let patience have her perfect work,
that ye may be perfect and entire, wanting nothing.
—James 1:4

Perfection is a seed. The life given in regeneration is a perfect life. Through ignorance and unbelief, the soul may never get beyond knowing that it has life. The soul may remain unconscious of what a wonderful, perfect life it has.

Perfection is a seed. It is a blessed hour when the soul wakes up to know this and, with a perfect heart, yields itself to appropriate all that God has given. The perfection of the perfect heart—a heart wholly yielded to seek God with all its strength—is again a seed, with infinite power of growth and increase.

Perfection is growth. As the Christian awakens to the consciousness of what God asks and gives, and maintains the vow of a wholehearted surrender, he grows in his sense of need and his trust in the promise of a divine life and strength. This continues until all the promises of grace come to a focus in the one assurance, *"But the God of all grace…[shall] make you perfect, stablish, strengthen, settle you"* (1 Peter 5:10). That faith, which was the fruit of previous growth, becomes the new seed of further growth. Perfection now develops into something riper and mellower. The overshadowing presence of Him who perfects rests abidingly on the spirit, and the whole character bears the impression of heavenliness and fellowship with the Unseen. The soul makes way for God and gives Him time to do His work. The God of peace, perfecting in every good work, gets entire possession it. This soul rests in the rest of God.

This does not take place over the course of a day. Perfection takes time. *"For ye have need of patience, that, after ye have done the will of God, ye might receive the promise"* (Hebrews 10:36). *"Be not slothful, but followers of them who through faith and patience inherit the promises"* (Hebrews 6:12). Man is a creature of time; he is under the law of development. In the kingdom of heaven, it is as it is in nature, from the seed comes first the blade, then the ear, then the full ear of corn. At times, there is nothing that is more mysterious to the believer than the slowness of God. It is as if our prayers are not heard, as if His promises are not fulfilled, as if our faith is in vain. And all the time God is hastening on with His work. He will avenge His own elect speedily, though He bears long with them.

We must let patience have its perfect work in us. We are so often impatient with ourselves, not content to trust God to do His work, that we hinder His work when we just want to hurry it. We are also impatient with God. Instead of trusting in Him, the God of peace, who is perfecting us, we worry ourselves because we do not see what we thought we would see for ourselves. But the law of faith is this: *"Rest in the Lord, and wait patiently for him"* (Psalm 37:7)—not only in times of abundance but especially in the path of perfection. Christians must have faith to an extent that very few realize. The assurance which rests in the unseen One who is working out its holy purpose will never be disappointed. As it has been said of an aged saint, "She was sure that, however long any soul might have to continue in the path of humiliation, with self-emptying, the end, with all who were faithful, would one day be a filling to overflowing of all their inward being with the presence of the holy One."

Let patience have its *"perfect work"* in us. This is the command. To those who obey it, the prospect held out is sure: *"that ye may be perfect and entire, wanting nothing"* (James 1:4). How words are heaped up to make us feel what the aim and expectation of the believer ought to be! We are to be *"perfect,"* something finished, that answers its end; *"entire,"* that every part might be in its place; and *"wanting nothing,"* other than all that the Father expects—such is the Christian character as God's Spirit sets it before us. There is a perfection which the Christian ought to regard as his duty and his life. Where patience has its perfect work, it will bring forth what the farmer longs for—fruit unto perfection. "God's work in man is the man. If God's teaching by patience has a perfect work in you, you are perfect."

But where there is to be this perfect fruit, there must first be the perfect seed. And that seed is the perfect heart. Without this, from what source could patience have its perfect work? With this, every trial, every difficulty, every failure is accepted as God's training school, and God is trusted as the faithful One, who is perfecting His own work. Let there first be the perfect heart that will lead to perfect patience, and that will then again lead to the fully perfected man.

Jesus Christ was not perfected in one day. It took time; in Him patience had its perfect work. True faith recognizes the need of time and rests in God. And time to us means days and years. Let us learn each day to renew the vow: "This day I will live for God as perfectly as His grace will enable me. This day

I will, in the patience of hope, trust the God of all grace, who Himself is perfecting me. This day I will be perfect and entire, wanting nothing." With such a vow renewed day by day, along with faith in Christ who *has* perfected us and God who *is* perfecting us, patience will do its perfect work. And we will become perfect and entire, wanting nothing.

25

THE PERFECT TONGUE

For in many things we all stumble.
If any stumbleth not in word, the same is a perfect man,
able to bridle the whole body also.
—James 3:2 (ASV)

There can be no perfection in art or science without attention to little things. One of the truest marks of genius is, in the presence of the highest ideal, the power to attend to even the smallest details. No chain is stronger than its feeblest link. The weakest point in the character of a Christian is the measure of his nearness to perfection. It is in the little things of daily life that perfection is attained and proved.

The tongue is a little member. A word of the tongue is such a little thing in the eyes of many. And yet we are told by our blessed Lord, *"By thy words thou shalt be justified"* (Matthew 12:37). When the Son of Man comes in the glory of His Father to render to every man according to his deeds, every word will be taken into account. In the light of the great day of God, if any man stumbles not in words, the same is a perfect man. This is the full-grown man, who has attained maturity, who has reached unto the measure of the stature of the fullness of Christ.

But is it possible for any man to be this perfect and not to stumble in a single word? Has James not just said, *"In many things we all stumble"* (James 3:2 ASV)? Just think of all the foolish words one hears among Christians—the sharp words, the hasty, thoughtless, unloving words—the words that are only half honest and not spoken from the heart. Think of all the sins of the tongue against the law of perfect love and perfect truth; and we must admit the terrible force of James' statement: *"In many things we all stumble"* (verse 2 ASV). When he adds, *"If any stumbleth not in word, the same is a perfect man"* (verse 2 ASV), can he really mean that God expects that we should live that way, and that we must seek and expect it, too?

Let us think. With what object does he use these words? In the beginning of his epistle, he spoke of patience having its perfect work in us, that we may be perfect and entire, wanting in nothing. There, entire perfection, with nothing wanting, is set before us as a definite promise to all who let patience do its perfect work in them. His epistle is written, as are all the epistles, under the painful impression of how far the ordinary Christian experience is from such perfection. But they are also written in the faith that it is not a hopeless task to teach God's people that they ought to be, that they can be, perfect and entire, wanting in nothing. Where James begins to speak of the tongue, the two sides of the truth again rise up before him. He expresses the ordinary experience in the general statement: *"In many things we all stumble"* (James 3:2 ASV). He sets forth the will of God and the power of grace in the blessed, and not impossible, ideal of all who seek to be perfect and entire: *"If any stumbleth not in word, the same is a perfect man"* (verse 2 ASV). James speaks of it in all simplicity, as a condition just as real as the other one of stumbling.

The question is again asked: Is it really a possible ideal? Does God expect it of us? Is grace promised for it? Let us call in Peter as a witness, and let us listen to what God's Spirit says through him about the terrible need of always stumbling, which some believe. Also, hear what he says about the blessed possibility of being kept from such stumbling. *"Give diligence,"* Peter writes, *"to make your calling and election sure: for if ye do these things, **ye shall never stumble**"* (2 Peter 1:10 ASV). *"Never"* includes not even in word. Let us hear what Jude says: *"Now unto him that is able to guard you from stumbling…through Jesus Christ our Lord, be glory, majesty, dominion and power, before all time, and now, and for evermore. Amen"* (Jude 1:24–25 ASV). It is the soul that knows and, without ceasing, trusts God as a God who guards from stumbling—a God who watches and keeps us every moment through Jesus Christ—that will, without ceasing, sing this song of praise.

These three texts above are the only ones in the New Testament in which the word *stumble* refers to the Christian life. Christ has said, *"According to your faith be it unto you"* (Matthew 9:29). If our faith feeds only and always on the Scripture *"In many things we all stumble"* (James 3:2 ASV), no wonder we do stumble. If with that *"stumble"* we remember the *"stumble not"* that follows, *"If any stumbleth not in word, the same is a perfect man"* (James 3:2 ASV), and the "not stumble" of Peter (see 2 Peter 1:10 ASV) and Jude (see James 3:2 ASV), the faith that embraces the promise will obtain it. God's power will translate it into our experience, and our life will be a living epistle into which God's words have been transcribed. Out of the abundance of the heart, the mouth speaks. (See Matthew 12:34; Luke 6:45.) Out of a heart that is perfect toward God—in which the love of God is shed abroad, in which Christ dwelleth—the tongue will bring forth words of truth and uprightness, love and gentleness, full of beauty and blessing. God wills it; God works it; so let us claim it.

26

GOD SHALL PERFECT YOU

And the God of all grace, who called you unto his eternal
glory in Christ, after that ye have suffered a little while,
shall himself perfect, establish, strengthen you. To him be
the dominion for ever and ever. Amen.
—1 Peter 5:10–11 (ASV)

The keynote of the first epistle of Peter is this: We move through suffering to glory. The word *suffer* occurs sixteen times, the word *glory* fourteen times. In Peter's closing words, he reminds the readers of all his teachings, as he writes, *"The God of all grace, who called you unto his eternal glory in Christ, after that ye have suffered a little while"* (1 Peter 5:10 ASV). In no epistle of the New Testament are the two aspects of Christ's death—His suffering for us and our suffering with Him to be like Him—so clearly and closely linked together. Fellowship with Christ—likeness to Christ, manifested in suffering—is the point of view from which Peter would have us look on life as the path to glory. To be a partaker of the sufferings and the glory of Christ is the Christian's privilege. Christ was perfected through suffering by God. The same God perfects us for suffering and glorifying Him in it.

"God…shall himself perfect…you" (1 Peter 5:10 ASV). In God alone is perfection. In Him is all perfection. And all perfection

comes from Him. When we consider the wondrous perfection there is in the sun, in the laws it obeys, and in the blessings it dispenses, and remember that it owes all to the will of the Creator, we acknowledge that its perfection is from God. Even so it is through the whole of nature—to the tiniest insect that floats in the sunbeam and the humblest little flower that basks in the light—everything owes its beauty to God alone. All His works praise Him. His works are perfect.

And do we not have here in nature the open secret of Christian perfection? It is God who must perfect us! *"God... shall himself perfect...you"* (1 Peter 5:10 ASV). What is revealed in nature is the pledge of what is secured to us in grace. *"It became him, for whom are all things, and by whom are all things, in bringing many sons unto glory, to make the captain of their salvation perfect through sufferings"* (Hebrews 2:10). It was appropriate for God to show that He is the God who works out perfection amid the weakness and suffering of a human life. This is what constitutes the very essence of salvation, to be perfected by God—to yield oneself to God, for whom and of whom are all things—trusting in Him to perfect us.

God has planted the desire after perfection deep in the heart of man. Is it not this desire for perfection that stirs the spirit of the artist and the poet, the discoverer and the inventor? Is it not the nearest possible approach to this perfection that awakens admiration and enthusiasm? And is it only in Christianity that all thought and all joy of present perfection is to be banished? Certainly not, if God's Word is true. The promise is sure and bright for our earthly life: *"God...shall himself perfect...you"* (1 Peter 5:10 ASV). Joined with the words, *"establish, strengthen you"* (verse 10 ASV), the *"himself perfect...you"* (verse 10 ASV) can refer to nothing but the present daily life. God will put you into the right position, and in that position, He will establish and strengthen you, so as to fit you perfectly for the life you have to live and the work you have to do.

We find it so hard to believe this, because we do not know what it means. Paul said, *"Ye are not under the law, but under grace"* (Romans 6:14). The law demands what we cannot give or do. Grace never asks what it does not give, and so the Father never asks what we cannot do. He Himself, who raised Jesus from the dead, is always ready to perfect us to do his will, in His resurrection power. Let us believe and be still until our soul is filled with the blessed truth, until we know that it will be done to us.

O brethren, learn to know this God, and claim Him—in His character—as yours: *"God...shall himself perfect...you"* (1 Peter 5:10 ASV)! Worship and adore Him, until your faith is filled with the assurance: My God Himself is perfecting me. Regard yourself as clay in the hands of the great Artist, who spends all His thought and time and love to make you perfect. Yield yourself in voluntary, loving obedience to His will and His Spirit. Yield yourself in full confidence to His very hands, and let the word ring through your whole being: *"God...shall himself perfect...you"* (verse 10 ASV). He will perfectly prepare you for all that He would have you do or be. Let every perfect bud or flower you meet whisper its message to you: only let God work; only wait upon Him. *"God...shall himself perfect...you"* (verse 10 ASV).

Believer, have you longed for this? O claim it; claim it now. Or rather, claim this God as your God now in very deed. Both the writer to the Hebrews and Peter in this epistle gathered up all their varied teachings into the one central promise, *"God... shall himself perfect...you"* (1 Peter 5:10 ASV). And there may come in the life of the believer a moment when he gathers up all his desires and efforts, all his knowledge of God's truth, and all his faith in God's promises. He will then concentrate them in the one simple act of surrender and trust, and, yielding himself wholly to do God's will, he will dare to claim God as the God that perfects him. And his life will become one doxology of adoring love: *"To him be the dominion for ever and ever. Amen"* (1 Peter 5:11 ASV).

27

KEEPING HIS WORD

But whoso keepeth his word,
in him verily is the love of God perfected.
—1 John 2:5

John Tauler, a German preacher, says of the apostle John, "In three ways, dear children, did the beloved Lord attract to Himself the heart of John.

"First, the Lord Jesus called him out of the world to make him an apostle.

"Next, He granted to him to rest upon His loving breast.

"Thirdly, and this was the greatest and most perfect nearness, on the holy day of Pentecost He gave him the Holy Spirit, and opened the door through which he should pass into the heavenly places.

"Thus, children, does the Lord first call you from the world and make you to be the messengers of God. And next, He draws you close to Himself, that you may learn to know His holy gentleness and lowliness, His deep and burning love, and His perfect unshrinking obedience.

"And yet this is not all. Many have been drawn thus far, and are satisfied to go no further. And yet they are far from the perfect nearness which the heart of Jesus desires.

"St. John lay at one moment on the breast of the Lord Jesus, and then he forsook Him and fled.

"If you have been brought so far as to rest on the breast of Christ, it is well. But yet there was to John a nearness still to come, one moment of which would be worth a hundred years of all that had gone before. The Holy Spirit was given to him—the door was opened.

"There is a nearness in which we lose ourselves, and God is all in all. This may come to us in one swift moment, or we may wait for it with longing hearts, and learn to know it at last. It was this St. Paul spoke of when he said that the thing which the heart has not conceived, God has now revealed to us by His Holy Spirit. The soul is drawn within the inner chamber, and there the wonders and the riches are revealed."[1]

To understand a writer, it is often necessary to know his or her character and history. When John wrote his gospel, he had been living in that innermost nearness—the inner chamber within the veil—of which Tauler speaks for fifty years. While on earth, Jesus had found in John a congenial spirit. John was receptive of His highest spiritual teaching, and Christ felt drawn to him in a special love. Now, at the writing of his gospel, John had spent fifty years in fellowship with the Son in the glory of the Father. He had experienced the power of the Holy Spirit to make the eternal, heavenly life of Jesus, in fellowship with the Father, an everyday reality. It is no wonder that when John testifies of his life as a life of perfect love, the church that is not living on this level can speak of it as only an ideal, one that is unattainable in this life. To one who thinks of what John was and what he knew of his Lord, as well as what a church under his teaching

1. Taken from *Three Friends of God* by Mrs. Bevan.

would be like, it is clear that the words are simply descriptive of the characters he saw around him. They were men to whom he could write,

> Beloved, if our heart condemn us not, then have we confidence toward God....Because we keep his commandments, and do those things that are pleasing in his sight.
>   (1 John 3:21–22)

> Whoso keepeth his word, in him verily is the love of God perfected.   (1 John 2:5)

John is the disciple whom *Jesus loved!* John had a special affinity to the words Jesus spoke to him about the love of God. The love with which Jesus loved him exercised its mighty influence. The Holy Spirit that came from the heart of the glorified Jesus intensified and spiritualized it all. And John became the Apostle of Love, who, gazing into the very depths of the divine glory and being, found that God is love. With this word, *love*, as the sum of his theology, he links the word *perfect*, found in the Old Testament and in the writings of his brother apostles. He tells us that this is perfection. The highest type of Christian character—the highest attainment of the Christian life—is for a man to have *God's love perfected in him.*

The condition and the mark of being perfected in love as Jesus taught him is this: *"If a man love me, he will keep my words: and my Father will love him, and we will come unto him, and make our abode with him"* (John 14:23). Keeping His Word—this is the link between the love of the disciple and the love of the Father. It leads to that wondrous union in which the Father's love draws Him to come and dwell in the loving heart. *"If ye keep my commandments,"* Jesus said, *"ye shall abide in my love; even as I* have kept my Father's commandments, and abide in his love" (John 15:10). And John confirms from his own experience what the Master spoke: *"Whoso keepeth his word, in him verily is the love of God perfected"* (1 John 2:5).

Thank God! This is a life to be found on earth: God's love can be perfected in us. Do not let what you see in the church around you make you doubt God's Word. When John spoke of perfect love and Paul of the love of God shed abroad in our hearts by the Holy Spirit, they testified from personal experience of what they had received in direct communication from the throne of glory. The words were to them the expression of a life of which we have little conception. To us, they convey no more truth than our low experience can put into them. Oh! that our hearts might be roused to believe in their heavenly, supernatural, fullness of meaning, and not to rest until we know that the love which passes all knowledge—that is, the love of God—the love of Christ, dwells within us as a fountain springing up unto everlasting life. *"The love of God perfected* [in us]" (1 John 2:5)—the prospect is sure to everyone who will allow the love of God in Christ to have the mastery in their lives and who will allow God to prove what He can do for those who love Him.

28

LOVING ONE ANOTHER

Beloved, if God so loved us, we ought also to love one
another. No man hath seen God at any time.
If we love one another, God dwelleth in us,
and his love is perfected in us.
—1 John 4:11–12

The first mark of a soul in whom the love of God is being perfected is this: keeping His Word. The path of obedience— the loving obedience of the perfect heart, the obedience of a life wholly given up to God's will—is the path the Son opened up into the presence and the love of the Father. It is the only path that leads to *perfect love*.

The commandments of Christ are all included in the word *love*, because *"love is the fulfilling of the law"* (Romans 13:10). *"A new commandment I give unto you, That ye love one another; as I have loved you"* (John 13:34). This is Christ's word: he who keeps this word keeps all the commandments. Love for the brethren is the second mark of a soul seeking to enter the life of *perfect love*.

In the very nature of things, it cannot be any other way. *"[Love] seeketh not her own"* (1 Corinthians 13:5). Love loses itself in going out to live in others. Love is the death of self. Where self still lives, there can be no thought of *perfect love*.

Love is the very being and glory of God. It is His nature and property, as He give of His own life to all His creatures, to communicate His own goodness and blessedness. The gift of His Son is the gift of Himself to be the life and joy of man. When that love of God enters the heart, it imparts its own nature—the desire to give itself to the very death for others. When the heart wholly yields itself to be transformed into His nature and likeness, then *love* takes possession of it. There the love of God is perfected.

The question is often asked whether it is the love of God to us, or our love to God, that is meant by *perfect love*. The words include both, because it implies a great deal more. The love of God is one, as God is one—His life, His very being. Where that love descends and enters, it retains its nature. It is always the divine life and love within us. God's love to us, our love to God and Christ, and our love to the brethren and to all men—all these are aspects of one and the same love. Just as there is one Holy Spirit in God and in us, so there is one divine love—the love of the Spirit—that dwells in God and in us.

To know this is a wonderful help to our faith. It teaches us that to love God or the brethren or our enemies is not a thing our efforts can attain. We can only do it because the divine love is dwelling in us, and only as far as we yield ourselves to the divine love as a living power within, as a life that has been born into us, a life that the Holy Spirit strengthens into action. Our part is first of all to rest, to cease from effort, to know that He is in us, and to give way to the love that dwells and works in us in a power that is from above.

How well John remembered the night when Jesus spoke so wonderfully of love in His parting words! Indeed, how impossible it appeared to the disciples to love as He had loved! How much there had been among them of pride and envy and selfishness; anything but love like His! How it had broken out among them that very night at the supper table! They never could love like the Master—it was impossible.

But what a change occurred when the risen One breathed on them and said, *"Receive ye the Holy Ghost"* (John 20:22). And how that change was consummated when the Holy Spirit came down from heaven, and out of that wonderful *love* which there flowed in holy interchange between the Father and the Son, when they met again in glory, the love of God was released in their hearts! In the love of the day of Pentecost, the perfect love celebrated its first great triumph in the hearts of men.

The love of God still reigns. The Spirit of God still waits to take possession of hearts where He has thus far had little room. He had been in the disciples all the time, but they had not known of what manner of spirit they were. He had come upon them on that evening when the risen One breathed upon them. But it was on Pentecost that He filled them so that love divine prevailed and overflowed, and they were perfected in love.

Let every effort we make to love, and every experience of how feeble our love is, lead us and draw us on to Jesus on the throne. In Him, the love of God is revealed and glorified and rendered accessible to us. Let us believe that the love of God can come down as a fire that will consume and destroy self and make loving one another—fervent, perfect love—the one mark of discipleship. Let us believe that this love of God, this perfect love, can be shed abroad in our hearts by the Holy Spirit who has been given to us, in a measure far beyond what we have now. Our tongues and lives, our homes and churches, will then prove to our sinful, perishing fellow men that there are still children of God in whom the love of God is perfected.

Even as Christian life has it stages, so love, too, has its two stages. There is love seeking, struggling, and doing its best to obey, and ever failing. And there is love finding, resting, rejoicing, and ever triumphing. This takes place when self and its efforts have been given into the grave of Jesus, and His life and love have taken their place. The birth of heavenly love in the soul has come. In the power of the heavenly life, to love is natural and easy. As Christ dwells in the heart, we are rooted and grounded in love, and we know the love that passes knowledge.

29

GOD DWELLING IN US

No man hath seen God at any time. If we love one another, God dwelleth in us, and his love is perfected in us. Hereby know we that we dwell in him, and he in us, because he hath given us of his Spirit.
—1 John 4:12–13

N*o man hath seen God at any time"* suggests there is a vision of God we may not yet have. The all-consuming, all-absorbing fire of God's glory—bringing death to all that is of nature—is not consistent with our earthly state. But an equivalent is given in its place that can prepare and train us for the beautiful vision to come, and also satisfy the soul with all that it can contain of God. We cannot see God, but we can have *"God dwell*[ing] *in us, and his love...perfected in us."* Though the brightness of God's glory is not to be seen, yet the presence of what is the very essence of that glory—His love—may now be known. God's love is perfected in us; God Himself abides in us; this is the heaven we can have on earth.

What is the way to this blessedness? *"God dwelleth in us, and his love is perfected in us"* when *"we love one another"* (1 John 4:12). We may not see God, but we see our brother. In him we have an object that will awaken and call forth the divine love within us. It will exercise and strengthen and develop that love, and it will open the way for the divine love to do its beloved work through us, to perfect us in love. It will awaken the divine contentment and draw it near to come within us and take up its abode there. In my brother, I have an object in which God calls me to prove all my love to Him. In loving my brother, however unlovely he may be, love proves that self no longer lives. It proves that it is a flame of the fire which consumed the Lamb of God. It shows that God's love is being perfected in us, and that it is God Himself who lives and loves within us.

"If we love one another, God dwelleth in us....Hereby know we that we dwell in him, and he in us, because he hath given us of his Spirit" (1 John 4:12–13). The wonderful knowledge that God abides in us and His love is perfected in us is not the result of reflection—a deduction from what we see in ourselves. No, divine things, divine love, the divine indwelling are only seen in divine light. *"Hereby know we that we dwell in him, and he in us, because he hath given us of his Spirit"* (verse 13). John remembers how little the disciples understood and experienced the words of Jesus until that never-to-be-forgotten day when, in the light of the fire that came from heaven, all became luminous and real. It is the Holy Spirit alone who accomplishes this in us. And it is not in His ordinary gracious workings, such as the disciples already had before that day, but in His special bestowment, direct from the throne of the exalted Jesus, that He becomes personally and permanently present to the soul that will rest content with nothing less. It is by the Holy Spirit's residence in our hearts that we know that God dwells in us, and we in Him, and that His love is perfected in us.

This is true in the Christian life now, even as it was then. It is the special work of the Holy Spirit to reveal the indwelling

God in us and to perfect us in love. By slow steps, we have to master first one side of truth and then another; to practice first one grace and then the very opposite. For a time, our whole heart goes all out in the aim to know and to do His will. Then again, it is as if there is only one thing to do—to love—and we feel as if in our own home, in all our dealings with men, in our outlook concerning the church and the world, we need only to practice love. After a time, we see how we fail, and we turn to the Word that calls us to faith, to cease from self, and to trust in Him who works both to will and to do. Here once more we come short. And next we feel that this alone can meet our need—a share in the Pentecostal gift—the Spirit given in power as never before. Let none faint or be discouraged. Let us seek to obey and to love and to trust with a perfect heart. In that in which we have attained, let us be faithful. But also let us press on to perfection. Let us confidently expect that this part of the Word will also be made all our own: *"If we love one another, God dwelleth in us, and his love is perfected in us. Hereby know we that we dwell in him, and he in us, because he hath given us of his Spirit"* (1 John 4:12–13).

It is only in the path of love—love in practical exercise, seeking to be perfect love—that this wonderful blessing can be found: God dwelling in us, and we in Him. And it is only by the Holy Spirit that we can know that we have it. God dwells in us, and His love is perfected in us. God is love; how sure it is that He longs to abide with us! God is love, who sends forth the Spirit of His Son to fill the hearts that are open to Him. How sure it is that we can be perfected in love! A perfect heart can count on being filled with a perfect love. Let nothing less than a perfect love be our aim so that we may have God abiding in us and His love perfected in us. We will know it by the Spirit which He has given to us.

30

BEING AS HE IS

*Herein is our love made perfect, that we may have
boldness in the day of judgment: because as he is,
so are we in this world.*
—1 John 4:17

Let us review the steps in the life of perfected love that have already been set before us. The divine love entering the heart manifests itself first in loving obedience to Christ. Of that obedience, love to the brethren in active exercise becomes the chief mark and manifestation. In this obedient love and loving obedience, the principle of fellowship with God—God abiding in us—is developed and strengthened. Of this fellowship, the Holy Spirit gives the evidence and abiding consciousness of His living in us. Such is the path in which love is perfected. Obedience to Christ; love to the brethren; the indwelling of God in us, and us in Him; the communication and revelation of all this by the Holy Spirit. All these are correlated ideas; they imply and condition each other. Together they make up the blessed life of perfect love.

The perfect heart began by seeking God wholly and alone. It found Him in the perfect way, through obedient love to the Lord, ministering to and loving the brethren. So it came in Christ to the Father, to fellowship with Him. So it was prepared and opened for that special illumination of the Spirit which revealed God's indwelling. The Father came to take up His abode. What was at first but a little seed—the perfect heart—has grown up and borne fruit. The perfect heart is now a heart in which the love of God is perfected. Love has taken full possession and reigns throughout the whole being.

Does the apostle John have anything more to say about perfect love? Yes, two things. He tells us its highest blessing: *"Herein is our love made perfect, that we may have boldness in the day of judgment"* (1 John 4:17). And the reason for this is *"because as he is, so are we in this world"* (verse 17). Let us here consider this second thought. It is in Christ that we are perfect. It is with the same perfection with which Christ was perfected Himself that He makes us perfect, that God now perfects us. Our place in Christ implies perfect unity of life and spirit, disposition and character. John gathers up all the elements of perfect love he has mentioned, and in view of the day of judgment, and the boldness that perfect love will give us, combines them together, saying, *"Because as he is, so are we in this world"* (1 John 4:17).

"As he is, so are we" (verse 17). In chapter two, he said, *"He that saith he abideth in him ought himself also so to walk, even as he walked"* (1 John 2:6). Likeness to Christ in His walk of obedience on earth is the mark of perfect love.

Then in chapter three we read, *"And every man that hath this hope in him* [the hope of being like Him, when we will see Him as He is] *purifieth himself, even as he is pure"* (1 John 3:3). Likeness to Christ in His heavenly purity is the mark of perfect love.

Then we read further, *"Hereby perceive we the love of God, because he laid down his life for us: and we ought to lay down our lives for the brethren"* (1 John 3:16). Likeness to Christ in His love to us is the mark of perfect love.

31

CASTING OUT FEAR

*There is no fear in love; but perfect love casteth out fear:
because fear hath torment. He that feareth is not made
perfect in love.*
—1 John 4:18

John Bengel, a German theologian, says that there are four
steps in the Christian life: "Serving God without fear or love;
with fear without love; with fear and love; with love without
fear." And Augustine says, "Fear prepares the way for love;
where there is no fear, there is no opening for love to enter." Fear
is the medicine, love the healing. Fear leads to love. When love
is perfected, fear is done. Perfect love casts out fear. *"Herein is
our love made perfect, that we may have boldness in the day of judgment: because as he is, so are we in this world"* (1 John 4:17).

The day of judgment! What a day that will be! Many have no
fear of that day, because they trust that they have been justified.
They imagine that the same grace which justified the ungodly
will give them passage into heaven. This is not what Scripture
teaches. The reality of our having obtained forgiveness will be
tested in that day by our having bestowed forgiveness on others.
Our fitness for entering the kingdom is determined by the way
in which we have served Jesus in the ministry of love to the sick

and the hungry. In our justification, all this had no part. In the judgment, it will be the all-important element. If we are to see Him as He is, and to be like Him, we must have purified ourselves as He is pure. It is perfect love—to be in this world even as He is—that casts out fear and gives us boldness in the day of judgment. He who fears is not made perfect in love. (See 1 John 4:18.)

The day of judgment! What a day! What a blessed thing to have boldness in that day! To meet the burning, fiery furnace of God's holiness, to be ready to be judged by our conformity to Christ's likeness and image, and to have no fear—what blessedness! It is this that makes what Scripture reveals of perfection, and of love perfected in us, of such immediate and vital interest to each one of us.

We have come to the close of our meditations on what Scripture teaches about the perfection attainable in this life. We began with the perfect heart, the heart wholly set upon God, as the mark of the man whom God counts a perfect man. We saw the perfect man walking in a perfect way, *"walking in all the commandments and ordinances of the Lord blameless"* (Luke 1:6). We found the standard at once infinitely arise in the New Testament. Perfect as the Father is the child's standard; perfected as the Master is the disciple's model; perfect in all the will of God is the Christian's aim and hope. And then to meet this high demand, the Word came to us: perfect in Christ, perfected by Christ, God Himself perfecting us in every good thing. And now John, the beloved disciple, has summed up all the teaching of the Word with this perfect love of which he speaks. Keeping Christ's Word, loving the brethren, abiding in God, staying filled with the Spirit, being even as Christ is, we can live perfected in love. With a heart that does not condemn us, we can have boldness before God, because we keep His commandments and do the things that are pleasing in His sight. With God's love perfected in us, we have boldness in the day of judgment.

Beloved fellow Christian! To have the love of God perfected in us, to be perfected in love, perfect love—these all are a divine possibility, a divine reality—the ripened fruit of the perfect life. We now know the tree on which this fruit grows. Its root is a heart perfect with God, walking before Him and being perfect. Let us be perfect in our surrender to Him in obedience and trust. Let the spirit of our daily life be characterized by deep dependence on Him, faith in Him, patient waiting on Him, and expecting all from Him alone. It is God Himself who must give it. Let us count on Him for nothing less than to be perfected in love and to have Him abiding in us. This is what He longs to do for us.

The tree that grows on this root is a life in union with Christ, aiming at perfect conformity to Him. Perfect in Christ, perfected by Christ, perfected by God like Christ and through Christ. When these words—pregnant with the will and love of God and the mystery of redemption—become the daily life of the soul, the perfect heart then rules the life, and the believer learns to stand perfect in all the will of God. The tree brings forth fruit abundantly.

Let us go on to perfection. Obedience and brotherly love, fellowship with God and likeness to Christ, and the unhindered flow and rule of the Holy Spirit, lead the soul into a life of perfect love. The God of love gets His heart's desire. The love of God celebrates its triumph. The days of heaven are begun on earth. The soul is perfected in love.

"Finally, brethren, farewell. Be perfect" (2 Corinthians 13:11). Be perfect with God. May you aim at nothing less. God will show Himself perfect to you. He will perfectly reveal Himself

to you and will perfectly possess you. Believe this. "*God...shall himself perfect...you*" (1 Peter 5:10 ASV), day by day. With each new morning, you may claim this. Live in surrender to His work and accept it. Do not fear and do not be discouraged. God Himself will grant you the knowledge of perfect love. "*God dwelleth in us, and his love is perfected in us*" (1 John 4:12).

ABOUT THE AUTHOR

Andrew Murray (1828–1917) was an amazingly prolific Christian writer. He lived and ministered as both a pastor and author in the towns and villages of South Africa. Some of Murray's earliest works were written to provide nurture and guidance to Christians, whether young or old in the faith; they were actually an extension of his pastoral work. Once books such as *Abide in Christ, Divine Healing,* and *With Christ in the School of Prayer* were written, Murray became widely known, and new books from his pen were awaited with great eagerness throughout the world.

He wrote to give daily practical help to many of the people in his congregation who lived out in the farming communities and could come into town for church services only on rare occasions. As he wrote these books of instruction, Murray adopted the practice of placing many of his more devotional books into thirty-one separate readings to correspond with the days of the month.

At the age of seventy-eight, Murray resigned from the pastorate and devoted most of his time to his manuscripts. He continued to write profusely, moving from one book to the next with an intensity of purpose and a zeal that few men of God have ever equaled. He often said of himself, rather humorously, that he was like a hen about to hatch an egg; he was restless and unhappy until he got the burden of the message off his mind.

During these later years, after hearing of pocket-sized paperbacks, Andrew Murray immediately began to write books to be published in that fashion. He thought it was a splendid way to have the teachings of the Christian life at your fingertips, where they could be carried around and read at any time of the day.

One source has said of Andrew Murray that his prolific style possesses the strength and eloquence that are born of deep earnestness and a sense of the solemnity of the issues of the Christian life. Nearly every page reveals an intensity of purpose and appeal that stirs men to the depths of their souls. Murray moves the emotions, searches the conscience, and reveals the sins and shortcomings of many of us with a love and hope born out of an intimate knowledge of the mercy and faithfulness of God.

For Andrew Murray, prayer was considered our personal home base from which we live our Christian lives and extend ourselves to others. During his later years, the vital necessity of unceasing prayer in the spiritual life came to the forefront of his teachings. It was then that he revealed the secret treasures of his heart concerning a life of persistent and believing prayer.

Countless people the world over have hailed Andrew Murray as their spiritual father and given credit for much of their Christian growth to the influence of his priceless devotional books.